Poverty in the United States: 2013

Thomas Gabe
Specialist in Social Policy

September 25, 2014

Congressional Research Service

7-5700

www.crs.gov

RL33069

CRS Report for Congress ————————————————————
Prepared for Members and Committees of Congress

Summary

In 2013, 45.3 million people were counted as poor in the United States under the official poverty measure—a number statistically unchanged from the 46.5 million people estimated as poor in 2012. The *poverty rate*, or percent of the population considered poor under the official definition, was reported at 14.5% in 2013, a statistically significant drop from the estimated 15.0% in 2012. Poverty in the United States increased markedly over the 2007-2010 period, in tandem with the economic recession (officially marked as running from December 2007 to June 2009), and remained unchanged at a post-recession high for three years (15.1% in 2010, and 15.0% in both 2011 and 2012). The 2013 poverty rate of 14.5% remains above a 2006 pre-recession low of 12.3%, and well above an historic low rate of 11.3% attained in 2000 (a rate statistically tied with a previous low of 11.1% in 1973).

The incidence of poverty varies widely across the population according to age, education, labor force attachment, family living arrangements, and area of residence, among other factors. Under the official poverty definition, an average family of four was considered poor in 2013 if its pre-tax cash income for the year was below $23,834.

The measure of poverty currently in use was developed some 50 years ago, and was adopted as the "official" U.S. statistical measure of poverty in 1969. Except for minor technical changes, and adjustments for price changes in the economy, the "poverty line" (i.e., the income thresholds by which families or individuals with incomes that fall below are deemed to be poor) is the same as that developed nearly a half century ago, reflecting a notion of economic need based on living standards that prevailed in the mid-1950s.

Moreover, poverty as it is currently measured only counts families' and individuals' pre-tax money income against the poverty line in determining whether or not they are poor. In-kind benefits, such as benefits under the Supplemental Nutrition Assistance Program (SNAP, formerly named the Food Stamp program) and housing assistance are not accounted for under the "official" poverty definition, nor are the effects of taxes or tax credits, such as the Earned Income Tax Credit (EITC) or Child Tax Credit (CTC). In this sense, the "official" measure fails to capture the effects of a variety of programs and policies specifically designed to address income poverty.

A congressionally commissioned study conducted by a National Academy of Sciences (NAS) panel of experts recommended, some 20 years ago, that a new U.S. poverty measure be developed, offering a number of specific recommendations. The Census Bureau, in partnership with the Bureau of Labor Statistics (BLS), has developed a Supplemental Poverty Measure (SPM) designed to implement many of the NAS panel recommendations. The SPM is to be considered a "research" measure, to supplement the "official" poverty measure. Guided by new research, the Census Bureau and BLS intend to improve the SPM over time. The "official" statistical poverty measure will continue to be used by programs that use it as the basis for allocating funds under formula and matching grant programs. The Department of Health and Human Services (HHS) will continue to issue poverty income guidelines derived from "official" Census Bureau poverty thresholds. HHS poverty guidelines are used in determining individual and family income eligibility under a number of federal and state programs. Estimates from the SPM differ from the "official" poverty measure and are presented in a final section of this report.

Contents

Figures

Tables

Appendixes

Contacts

Trends in Poverty[1]

In 2013, the official U.S. poverty rate was 14.5%, compared to 15.0% in 2012, and marked the first statistically significant drop in the rate since 2006. In 2013, 45.3 million persons were estimated as having income below the official poverty line, a number statistically unchanged from the estimated 46.5 million poor in 2012. (See **Figure 1**.)

Figure 1 shows a clear relationship between poverty and the economy. The level of poverty tends to follow the economic cycle quite closely, tending to rise when the economy is faltering and fall when the economy is in sustained growth.

The poverty rate increased markedly over the past decade, in part a response to two economic recessions (periods marked in red). A strong economy during most of the 1990s is generally credited with the declines in poverty that occurred over the latter half of that decade, resulting in a record-tying, historic low poverty rate of 11.3% in 2000 (a rate statistically tied with the previous lowest recorded rate of 11.1% in 1973). The poverty rate increased each year from 2001 through 2004, a trend generally attributed to economic recession (March 2001 to November 2001), and failed to recede appreciably before the onset of the December 2007 recession. This most recent recession, which officially ended in June 2009, was the longest recorded (18 months) in the post-World War II period.[2] Over the course of the most recent recession, the unemployment rate increased from 4.9% (January 2008) to 7.2% (December 2008), and continued to rise over most of 2009, peaking at 10.0% in October of that year. Even as the economy has been recovering, poverty has remained well above pre-recessionary levels. Although the unemployment rate has generally been falling since late 2009, it has not been until this past year that we've seen a marked (statistically significant) decline in the official poverty rate. That the unemployment rate has continued to fall over 2014 suggests that poverty levels are likely to fall in 2014. Poverty statistics for 2014 poverty will be issued in the late summer of 2015. The recession especially affected non-aged adults (persons age 18 to 64) and children. (See **Figure 2**.) The poverty rate of non-aged adults reached 13.8% in 2010, the highest it has been since the early 1960s.[3] In 2013 the non-aged poverty rate of 13.6% remained statistically unchanged from rates seen in the prior three years. The poverty rate for non-aged adults will need to fall to 10.8% to reach its 2006 pre-recession level.

The 2013 poverty data provide one encouraging sign with respect to children. Both the estimated number of poor children and their poverty rate fell from 2012 to 2013. In 2013, the number of poor children fell by an estimated 1.3 million (15.4 million in 2012 to 14.1 million in 2013), and their poverty rate fell from 21.3% in 2012 to 19.5% in 2013. The 2013 child poverty rate is still well above its pre-recession low of 16.9% (2006). Child poverty appears to be especially sensitive to economic cycles, as it often takes two working parents to support a family, and a loss of work by one may put the family at risk of falling into poverty.[4] Moreover, roughly one-third of all

---

[1] Supporting data are based on the following: U.S. Census Bureau, Income and Poverty in the United States: 2013; Current Population Report No. P60-249, September 2014; and unpublished Census Bureau tables, available on the Internet at http://www.census.gov/hhes/www/poverty/data/incpovhlth/2013/index html.

[2] Periods of recession are officially defined by the National Bureau of Economic Research (NBER) Business Cycle Dating Committee. See http://www.nber.org/cycles/main.html.

[3] The poverty rate of non-aged adults was 17.0% in 1959. Comparable estimates are not available from 1960 through 1965. By 1966, the non-aged poverty rate stood at 10.5%. See **Table A-1**.

[4] CRS Report RL33615, *Parents' Work and Family Economic Well-Being*, by Thomas Gabe and Gene Falk.

---

children in the country live with only one parent, making them even more prone to falling into poverty when the economy falters.

In 2013, the aged poverty rate (9.5%) was statistically unchanged from 2012, although the number of poor rose by an estimated 305,000 (from 3.9 million in 2012 to 4.2 million in 2013). In spite of the recession, the aged poverty rate remains near an historic low level. The longer-term secular trend in poverty has been affected by changes in household and family composition and by government income security and transfer programs. In 1959, over one-third (35.2%) of persons age 65 and over were poor, a rate well above that of children (26.9%). Social Security, in combination with a maturing pension system, has helped greatly to reduce the incidence of poverty among the aged over the years, and as recent evidence seems to show, it has helped protect them during the economic downturn.

The U.S. "Official" Definition of Poverty[5]

The Census Bureau's poverty thresholds form the basis for statistical estimates of poverty in the United States.[6] The thresholds reflect crude estimates of the amount of money individuals or families, of various size and composition, need per year to purchase a basket of goods and services deemed as "minimally adequate," according to the living standards of the early 1960s. The thresholds are updated each year for changes in consumer prices. In 2013, for example, the average poverty threshold for an individual living alone was $11,888; for a two-person family, $15,142; and for a family of four, $23,834.[7]

The current official U.S. poverty measure was developed in the early 1960s using data available at the time. It was based on the concept of a minimal standard of food consumption, derived from research that used data from the U.S. Department of Agriculture's (USDA's) 1955 Food Consumption Survey. That research showed that the average U.S. family spent one-third of its pre-tax income on food. A standard of food adequacy was set by pricing out the USDA's Economy Food Plan—a bare-bones plan designed to provide a healthy diet for a temporary period when funds are low. An overall poverty income level was then set by multiplying the food plan by three, to correspond to the findings from the 1955 USDA Survey that an average family spent one-third of its pre-tax income on food and two-thirds on everything else.

The "official" U.S. poverty measure[8] has changed little since it was originally adopted in 1969, with the exception of annual adjustments for overall price changes in the economy, as measured by the Consumer Price Index for all Urban Consumers (CPI-U). Thus, the poverty line reflects a

---

[5] For a more complete discussion of the U.S. poverty measure, see CRS Report R41187, *Poverty Measurement in the United States: History, Current Practice, and Proposed Changes*, by Thomas Gabe.

[6] The Department of Health and Human Services (HHS) releases poverty income guidelines that are derived directly from Census poverty thresholds. These guidelines, a simplified approximation of the Census poverty thresholds, are used by HHS and other federal agencies for administering programs, particularly for determining program eligibility. For current guidelines and methods for their computation, see http://aspe hhs.gov/poverty/index.shtml.

[7] See http://www.census.gov/hhes/www/poverty/data/threshld/index html.

[8] The poverty measure was adopted as the "official poverty measure" by a directive issued in 1969 by the Bureau of the Budget, now the Office of Management and Budget (OMB). The directive was revised in 1978 to include revisions to poverty thresholds and procedures for updating thresholds for inflation using the Consumer Price Index (CPI). See OMB Statistical Policy Directive 14, available on the Internet at http://www.census.gov/hhes/povmeas/methodology/ombdir14 html.

measure of economic need based on living standards that prevailed in the mid-1950s. It is often characterized as an "absolute" poverty measure, in that it is not adjusted to reflect changes in needs associated with improved standards of living that have occurred over the decades since the measure was first developed. If the same basic methodology developed in the early 1960s was applied today, the poverty thresholds would be over three times higher than the current thresholds.[9]

Persons are considered poor, for statistical purposes, if their family's countable money income is below its corresponding poverty threshold. Annual poverty estimates are based on a Census Bureau household survey (Annual Social and Economic Supplement to the Current Population Survey, CPS/ASEC, conducted February through April). The official definition of poverty counts most sources of money income received by families during the prior year (e.g., earnings, social security, pensions, cash public assistance, interest and dividends, alimony, and child support, among others). For purposes of officially counting the poor, noncash benefits (such as the value of Medicare and Medicaid, public housing, or employer provided health care) and "near cash" benefits (e.g., food stamps, renamed Supplemental Assistance Nutrition (SNAP) benefits beginning in FY2009) are not counted as income, nor are tax payments subtracted from income, nor are tax credits added (e.g., Earned Income Tax Credit (EITC)). Many believe that these and other benefits should be included in a poverty measure so as to better reflect the effects of government programs on poverty.

The Census Bureau, in partnership with the Bureau of Labor Statistics (BLS), has recently released a Supplemental Poverty Measure (SPM), designed to address many of the perceived flaws of the "official" measure. The SPM is discussed in a separate section at the end this report (see "The Research Supplemental Poverty Measure").

---

[9] Based on U.S. Department of Labor Bureau of Labor Statistics Consumer Expenditure Survey data, in 2013 the average family spent an estimated 10.3% of pre-tax income on food (including food consumed at home and away from home), as opposed to one-third in the mid-1950s. This implies that the multiplier for updating poverty thresholds based on food consumption would be 9.7 (i.e., 1/0.103), or 3.2 times the multiplier of 3 subsumed under poverty thresholds developed in the 1960s. Author's calculations from http://www.bls.gov/cex/2013/aggregate/age.pdf.

Figure 1. Trend in Poverty Rate and Number of Poor Persons: 1959-2013, and Unemployment Rate from January 1959 through August 2014

(recessionary periods marked in red)

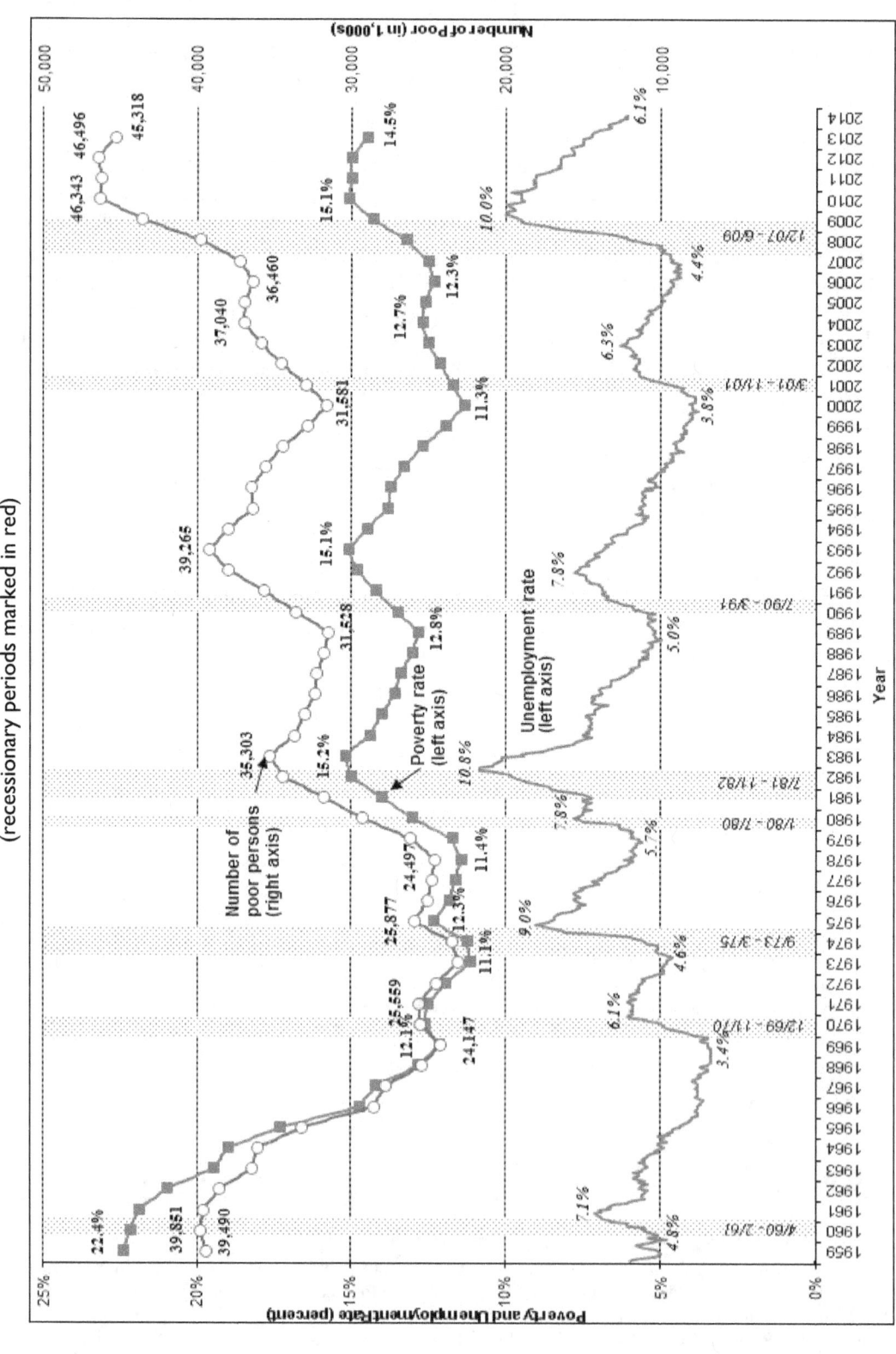

Source: Prepared by the Congressional Research Service (CRS) using U.S. Census Bureau, "Income and Poverty United States: 2013," Table B-1, Current Population Report P60-249, September 2014 available on the Internet at http://www.census.gov/content/dam/Census/library/publications/2014/demo/p60-249.pdf. Unemployment rates are available on the Internet at http://www.bls.gov/cps/. Recessionary periods defined by National Bureau of Economic Research Business Cycle Dating Committee: http://www.nber.org/cycles/main.html.

Figure 2. U.S. Poverty Rates by Age Group, 1959-2013

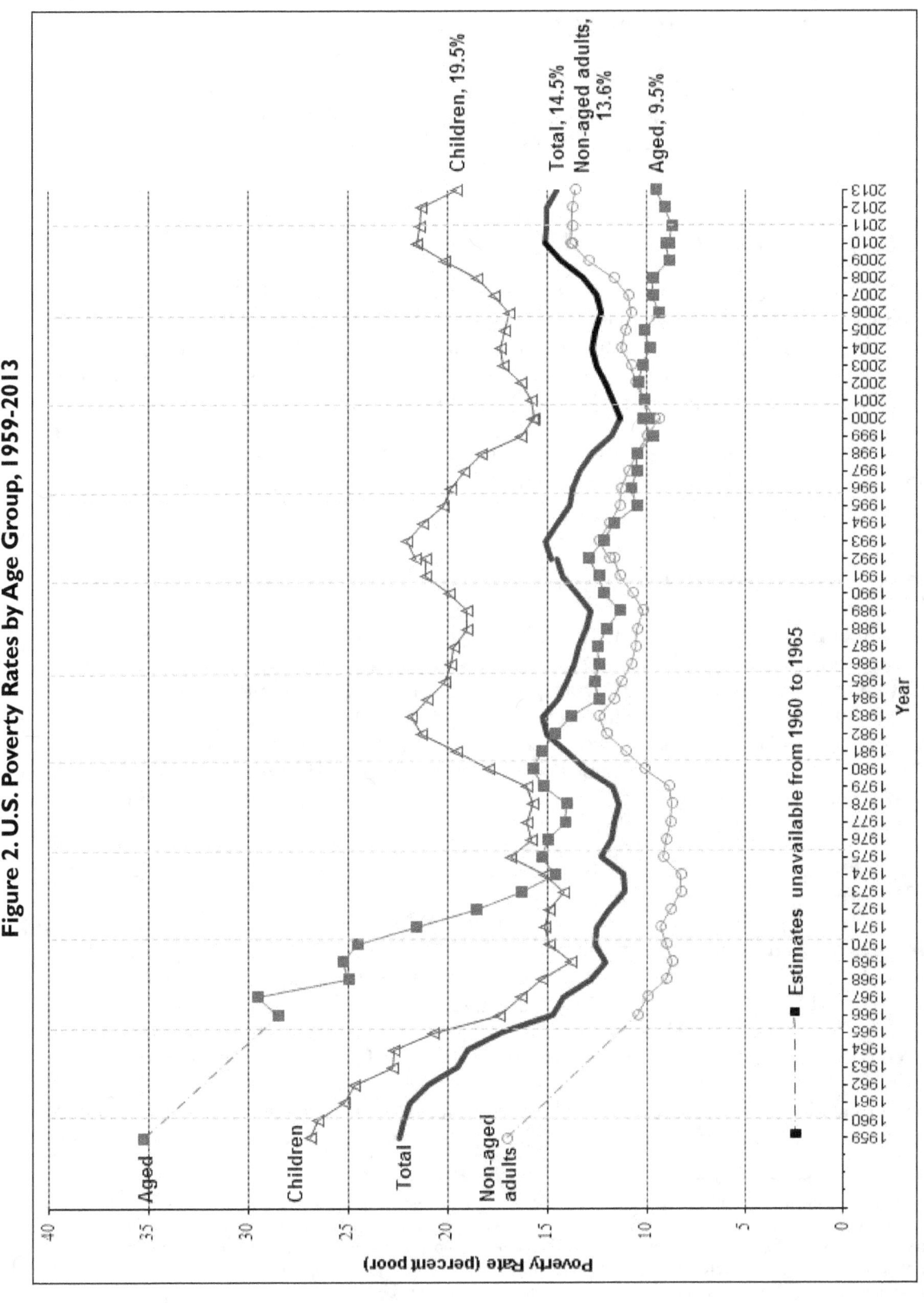

Source: Prepared by the Congressional Research Service using U.S. Census Bureau, "Income and Poverty in the United States: 2013," Tables B-1 and B-2, Current Population Report P60-249, September 2014, available on the Internet at http://www.census.gov/content/dam/Census/library/publications/2014/demo/p60-249.pdf.

Poverty among Selected Groups

Even during periods of general prosperity, poverty is concentrated among certain groups and in certain areas. Minorities; women and children; the very old; the unemployed; and those with low levels of educational attainment, low skills, or disability, among others, are especially prone to poverty.

Racial and Ethnic Minorities[10]

The incidence of poverty among African Americans and Hispanics exceeds that of whites by several times. In 2013, 27.2% of blacks (11.0 million) and 23.5% of Hispanics (12.7 million) had incomes below poverty, compared to 9.6% of non-Hispanic whites (18.8 million) and 10.5% of Asians (1.8 million). Although blacks represent only 13.0% of the total population, they make up 24.4% of the poor population; Hispanics, who represent 17.3% of the population, account for 28.1% of the poor. Poverty rates for Hispanics fell from 25.6% in 2012 to 23.5% in 2013, as did the number of poor Hispanics, from 13.6 million in 2012, to 12.7 million in 2013. Poverty rates and the numbers estimated as poor were statistically unchanged from 2012 to 2013 for white non-Hispanics, blacks, and Asians.

Nativity and Citizenship Status

In 2013, among the native-born population, 13.9% (37.9 million) were poor—a rate and number statistically unchanged from 2012 (14.3%, 38.8 million). Among the foreign-born population, 18.0% (7.4 million) were poor in 2013—a statistically significant drop in the poverty rate (from 19.7%), but not in the number estimated as poor. The poverty rate among foreign-born naturalized citizens (12.7%, in 2013) was lower than that of the native-born U.S. population (13.9%). In 2013, the poverty rate of non-citizens (22.8%) dropped significantly from 2012 (24.9%), as did the estimated number who were poor (about one-half million, dropping from 5.4 million in 2012, to 4.0 million in 2013).

Children

Poverty among children dropped significantly from 2012 to 2013. Their estimated poverty rate fell from 21.3% in 2012, to 19.5% in 2013. In 2013, an estimated 1.3 million fewer children were poor than in 2012 (14.1 million versus 15.4 million, respectively). However, the 2013 child poverty rate (19.5%) is still well above its pre-recession low of 16.9% (2006).. The lowest recorded rate of child poverty was in 1969, when 13.8% of children were counted as poor.

Children living in single female-headed families are especially prone to poverty. In 2013 a child living in a single female-headed family was nearly five times more likely to be poor than a child

---

[10] Beginning with the March 2003 CPS, the Census Bureau allows survey respondents to identify themselves as belonging to one or more racial groups. In prior years, respondents could select only one racial category. Consequently, poverty statistics for different racial groups for 2002 and after are not directly comparable to earlier years' data. The terms black and white, above, refer to persons who identified with only a single racial group. The term Hispanic refers to individuals' ethnic, as opposed to racial, identification. Hispanics may be of any race.

living in a married-couple family. In 2013, among all children living in single female-headed families, 45.8% were poor. In contrast, among children living in married-couple families, 9.5% were poor. The increased share of children who live in single female-headed families has contributed to the high overall child poverty rate. In 2013, one quarter (25.0%) of children were living in single female-headed families, more than double the share who lived in such families when the *overall* child poverty rate was at a historical low (1969). Among all poor children, nearly six in ten (58.7%) were living in single female-headed families in 2013.

In 2013, 38.0% of black children were poor (4.2 million), compared to 30.0% of Hispanic children (5.3 million) and 10.1% of non-Hispanic white children (3.8 million). (See **Figure 3**.) Among children living in single female-headed families, more than half of black children (54.0%) and Hispanic children (52.3%) were poor; in contrast, one-third of non-Hispanic white children (33.6%) were poor. The poverty rate among Hispanic children who live in married-couple families (19.9%) was above that of black children (16.8%), and four times that of non-Hispanic white children (4.9%) who live in such families. Contributing to the high rate of overall black child poverty is the large share of black children who live in single female-headed families (54.0%) compared to Hispanic children (30.1%) or non-Hispanic white children (15.7%). (See **Figure 4**.)

Figure 3. Child Poverty Rates by Family Living Arrangement, Race and Hispanic Origin, 2013

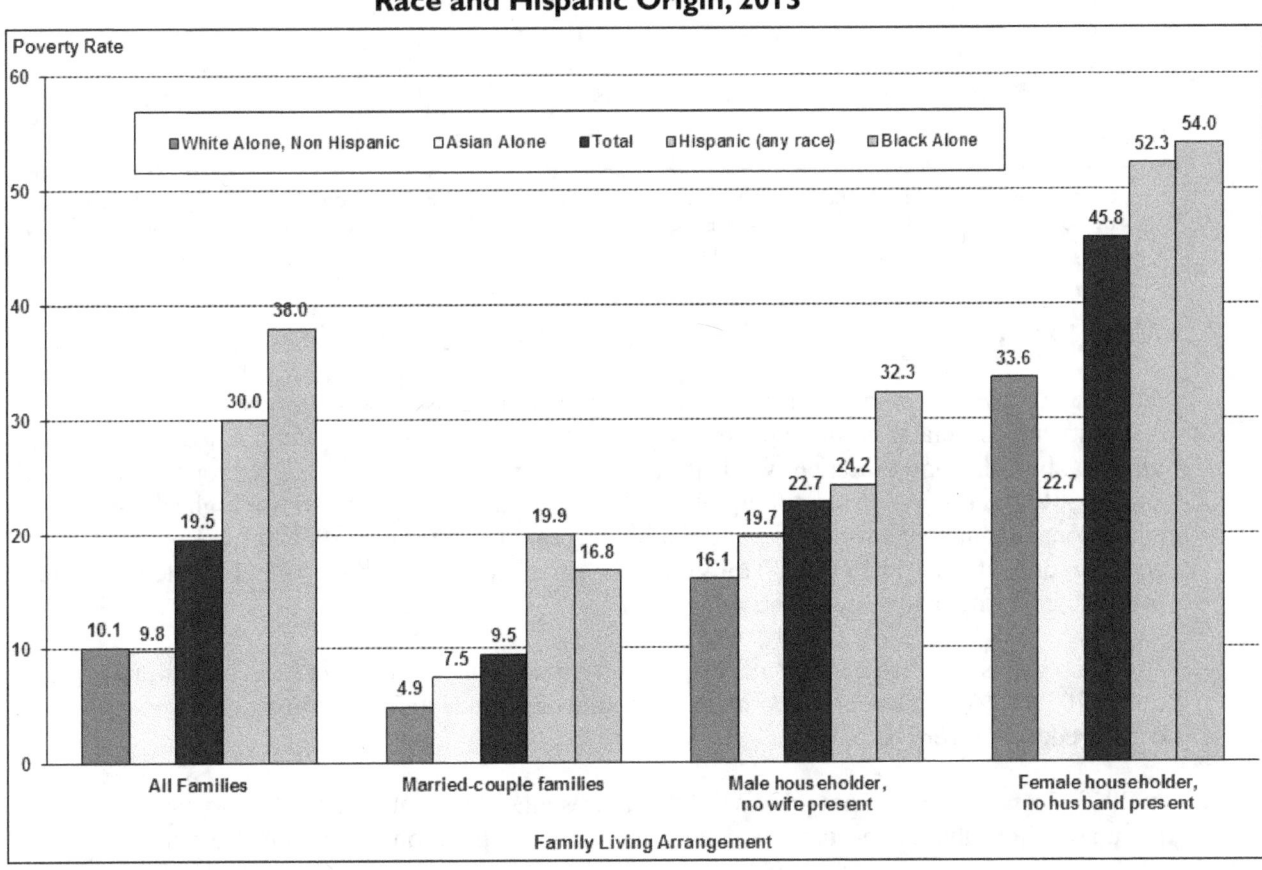

Source: Figure prepared by the Congressional Research Service (CRS) based on U.S. Census Bureau data from the 2014 Current Population Survey Annual Social and Economic Supplement, available at http://www.census.gov/hhes/www/cpstables/032014/pov/pov05_000.htm.

Figure 4. Composition of Children, by Family Type, Race and Hispanic Origin, 2013

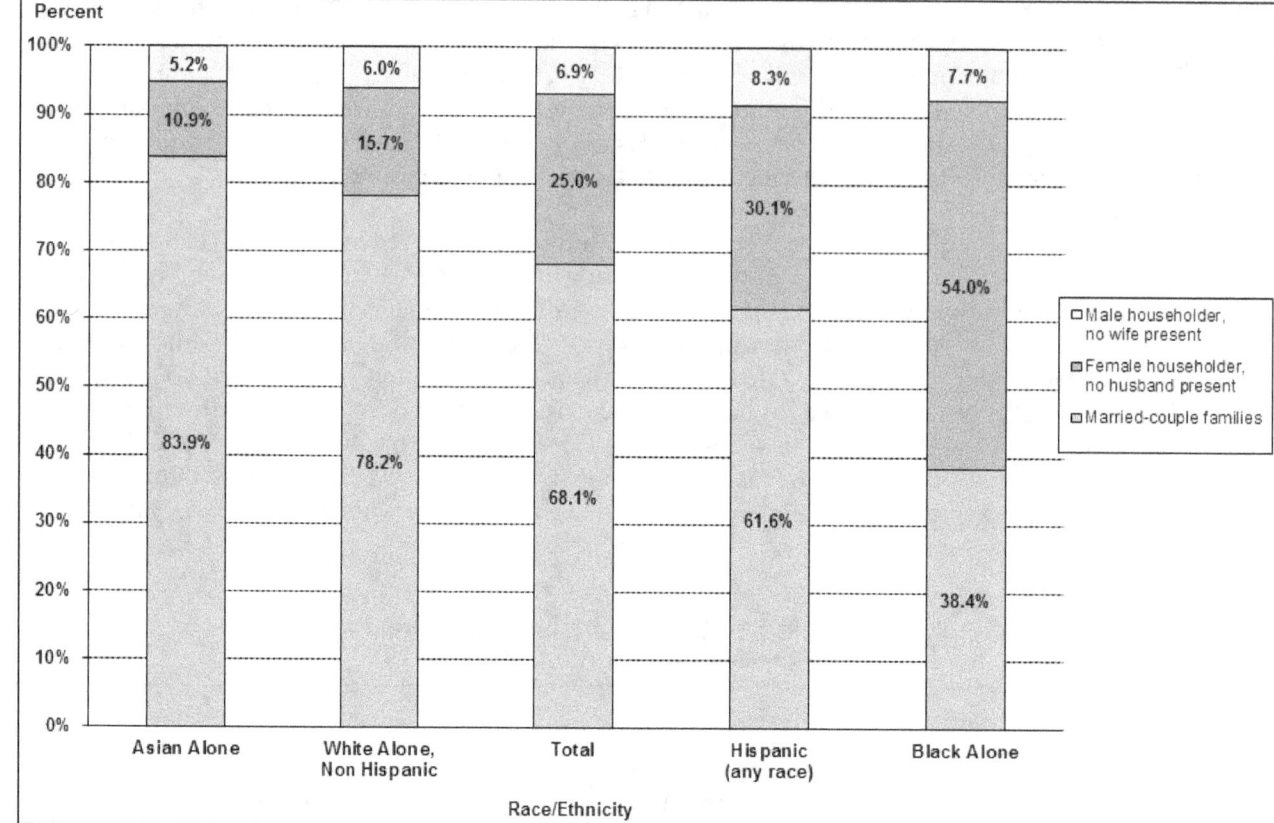

Source: Figure prepared by the Congressional Research Service (CRS) based on U.S. Census Bureau data from the2014 Current Population Survey Annual Social and Economic Supplement, available athttp://www.census.gov/hhes/www/cpstables/032014/pov/pov05_000.htm.

Adults with Low Education, Unemployment, or Disability

Adults with low education, those who are unemployed, or those who have a work-related disability are especially prone to poverty. Among 25- to 34-year-olds without a high school diploma, between one-third and two-fifths (36.8%) were poor in 2013. In 2013, one-in-ten 25- to 34-year-olds lacked a high school diploma. Within the same age group whose highest level of educational attainment was a high school diploma, about one in five (20.7%) were poor. In contrast, only about 1 in 16 (6.5%) of 25- to 34-year-olds with at least a bachelor's degree were found to be living below the poverty line.

Among persons between the ages of 16 and 64 who were unemployed in March 2014, nearly 3 out of 10 (29.8%) were poor based on their families' incomes in 2013; among those who were employed, 6.9% were poor.

In 2013, persons who had a work disability[11] represented 11.3% of the 16- to 64-year-old population, and about one-quarter (26.0%) of the poor population within this age range. Among

---

[11] The CPS asks several questions to determine whether individuals are considered to have a work disability. Persons are identified as having a work disability if they (1) reported having a health problem or disability that prevents them (continued...)

those with a severe work disability, 35.6% were poor, compared to 17.0% of those with a less severe disability and 11.4% who reported having no work-related disability.

The Aged

In 2013, the 9.5% poverty rate among persons age 65 and older, was statistically unchanged from the 2012 rate (9.1%), but statistically higher than the all-time low-poverty rate among the aged of 8.7% attained in 2011. The number of aged poor grew by 305 thousand from 2012 to 2013, from 3.9 million to 4.2 million,. Among persons age 75 and over, 11.2% were poor in 2013, compared to 8.3% of those ages 65 to 74. Measured by a slightly raised poverty standard (125% of the poverty threshold), 15.1% of the aged could be considered poor or "*near poor*" in 2013; 12.6% who are ages 65 to 74, and 18.4% who are 75 years of age and over, could be considered poor or "near poor."

Receipt of Need-Tested Assistance Among the Poor

In 2013, nearly three of every four poor persons (73.8%) lived in households that received any means-tested assistance during the year.[12] Such assistance could include cash aid, such as Temporary Assistance for Needy Families (TANF), Supplemental Security Income (SSI) payments, SNAP benefits (Food Stamps), Medicaid, subsidized housing, free or reduced price school lunches, and other programs. In 2013, somewhat over one in five (17.4%) poor persons lived in households that received *cash aid*; half (49.5%) received SNAP benefits (formerly named Food Stamps); six in ten (61.3%) lived in households where one or more household members were covered by Medicaid; and about one in seven (14.8%) lived in subsidized housing. Poor single-parent families with children are among those families most likely to receive cash aid. Among poor children who were living in single female-headed families, about one-fifth (21.9%) were in households that received government cash aid in 2013, down from 24.0% in 2012. The share of poor children in single female-headed families receiving cash aid is well below historical levels. In 1993, 70.2% of these children's families received cash aid. In 1995, the year prior to passage of sweeping welfare changes under PRWORA, 65% of such children were in families receiving cash aid.

The Geography of Poverty

Poverty is more highly concentrated in some areas than in others; it is about twice as high in center cities as it is in suburban areas and nearly three times as high in the poorest states as it is in the least poor states. Some neighborhoods may be characterized as having high concentrations of

---

(...continued)

from working or that limits the kind or amount of work they can do; (2) ever retired or left a job for health reasons; (3) did not work in the survey week because of long-term physical or mental illness or disability which prevents the performance of any kind of work; (4) did not work at all in the previous year because they were ill or disabled; (5) are under 65 years of age and covered by Medicare; (6) are under age 65 years of age and a recipient of Supplemental Security Income (SSI); or (7) received veteran's disability compensation. Persons are considered to have a severe work disability if they meet any of the criteria in (3) through (6), above. See http://www.census.gov/hhes/www/disability/disabcps.html.

[12] See http://www.census.gov/hhes/www/cpstables/032014/pov/pov26_000.htm

---

poverty. Among the poor, the likelihood of living in an area of concentrated or extreme poverty varies by race and ethnicity.

Poverty in Metropolitan and Nonmetropolitan Areas, Center Cities, and Suburbs

Within metropolitan areas, the incidence of poverty in central city areas is considerably higher than in suburban areas—19.1% versus 11.1%, respectively, in 2013. Nonmetropolitan areas had a poverty rate of 16.1%. A typical pattern is for poverty rates to be highest in center city areas, with poverty rates dropping off in suburban areas, and then rising with increasing distance from an urban core. In 2013, only nonmetropolitan areas experienced a statistically significant decline in poverty (both rate and numbers poor) from 2012, with the poverty rate decreasing from the 17.7% in 2012 to 16.1% in 2013, and the number of poor declining by an estimated 891 thousand persons. Poverty rates and estimated numbers of poor people remained statistically unchanged in metropolitan areas, center cities, and suburbs from 2012 to 2013.

Poverty by Region

In 2013, poverty rates were lowest in the Northeast (12.7%) and Midwest (1.2.9%), followed by the West (14.7%), and the South (16.1%) having the highest poverty rate. Poverty remained statistically unchanged (measured both in terms of numbers poor and rates) in each of the four regions from 2012 to 2013.

State Poverty Rates

American Community Survey (ACS) State Poverty Estimates—2013

Up to this point, the poverty statistics presented in this report come from the U.S. Census Bureau's Annual Social and Economic Supplement (ASEC) to the Current Population Survey (CPS). For purposes of producing state and sub-state poverty estimates, the Census Bureau now recommends using the American Community Survey (ACS)— because of its much larger sample size, the ACS produces estimates with a much smaller margin of statistical error than that of the CPS/ASEC. However, it should be noted that the ACS survey design differs from the CPS/ASEC in a variety of ways, and may produce somewhat different estimates than those obtained from the ASEC/CPS. Based on the 2013 ACS, the U.S. poverty rate was estimated to be 15.8%, compared to 14.5% based on the 2014 CPS/ASEC. The CPS/ASEC estimates are based on a survey conducted in February through April 2013, and account for income reported for the previous year. In contrast, the ACS estimates are based on income information collected between January and December 2013, for the prior 12 months. For example, for the sample with data collected in January, the reference period is from January 2012 to December 2013, and for the sample with data collected in December, from December 2012 to November 2013. The ACS data consequently cover a time span of 23 months, with the data centered at mid-December 2012.

Based on 2012 American Community Survey (ACS) data, poverty rates were highest in the South (with the exception of Virginia), extending across to Southwestern states bordering Mexico (Texas, New Mexico, and Arizona). (See **Figure 5**.) Poverty rates in several states bordering the Ohio River (Ohio, West Virginia, Kentucky) also exceeded the national rate, as did those of

Michigan and New York, and the District of Columbia, in the eastern half of the nation, and California, Oregon, and Montana in the western half.

States along the Atlantic Seaboard from Virginia northward tended to have poverty rates well below the national rate, as did three contiguous states in the upper Midwest/plains (Iowa, Minnesota, and North Dakota), as well as Utah, Wyoming, Alaska, and Hawaii.

Figure 5. Percentage of People in Poverty in the Past 12 Months by State and Puerto Rico: 2013

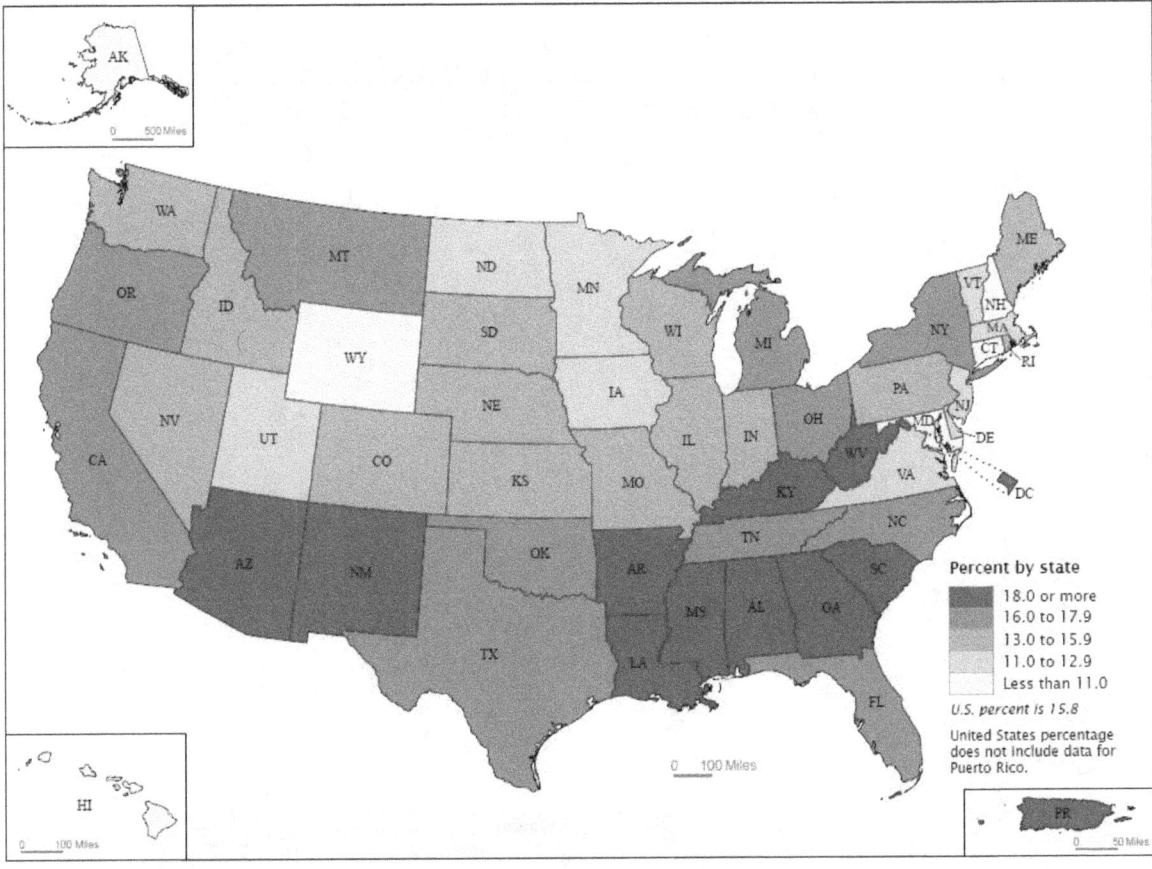

Source: U.S. Census Bureau, 2012 American Community Survey, 2013 Puerto Rico Community Survey. Alemayehu Bishaw, *Poverty: 2012 and 2013*, U.S. Census Bureau, American Community Survey Briefs, ACSBR/13-0101, Washington, DC, September 2014, p. 4, http://census.gov/content/dam/Census/library/publications/2014/acs/acsbr13-01.pdf.

Figure 6 shows estimated poverty rates for the United States and for each of the 50 states and the District of Columbia on the basis of the 2013 American Community Survey (ACS), the most recent ACS data currently available. In addition to the point estimates, the figure displays a 90% statistical confidence interval around each state's estimate, indicating the degree to which these estimates might be expected to vary based on sample size. Although the states are sorted from lowest to highest by their respective poverty rate point estimates, the precise ranking of each state is not possible because of the depicted margin of error around each state's estimate. All states with non-overlapping statistical confidence intervals have statistically significant different poverty rates from one another. Some states with overlapping confidence intervals may also have significantly different poverty rates from one another, measured at the 90% confidence interval.[13] For example, New Hampshire, shown as having the lowest poverty rate (8.7%) in 2013, is statistically tied with Alaska (9.3%). Mississippi clearly stands out as the state with the highest poverty rate (24.0%) and New Mexico, with a poverty rate of 21.8%, has the second-highest poverty rate. Louisiana, a state ranked as having the third-highest poverty rate (19.7%), is statistically tied with Arkansas (19.7%) and the District of Columbia (18.9%), but not with Georgia (19.0%), even though Louisiana and Georgia's statistical confidence intervals overlap.

---

[13] Two states' poverty rates are statistically different at the 90% statistical confidence interval if the confidence intervals bounding their respective poverty rates do not overlap with one another. However, some states with overlapping confidence intervals may also statistically differ at the 90% statistical confidence interval. In order to precisely determine whether two states' poverty rates differ from one another, a statistical test of differences must be performed. The standard error for the difference between two estimates may be calculated as: $SE_{StateA} - SE_{StateB} = \sqrt{SE_{StateA}^2 + SE_{StateB}^2}$. Two estimates are considered statistically different if at the 90% statistical confidence interval the absolute value of the difference is greater than 1.645 times the standard error of the difference (i.e., $|Povrate_{StateA} - Povrate_{StateB}| > 1.645x(SE_{StateA} - SE_{StateB})$.

Note that the standard error for a state's poverty estimate may be obtained by dividing the margin of error depicted in **Figure 6** by 1.645.

Figure 6. Poverty Rates for the 50 States and the District of Columbia: 2013 American Community Survey (ACS) Data

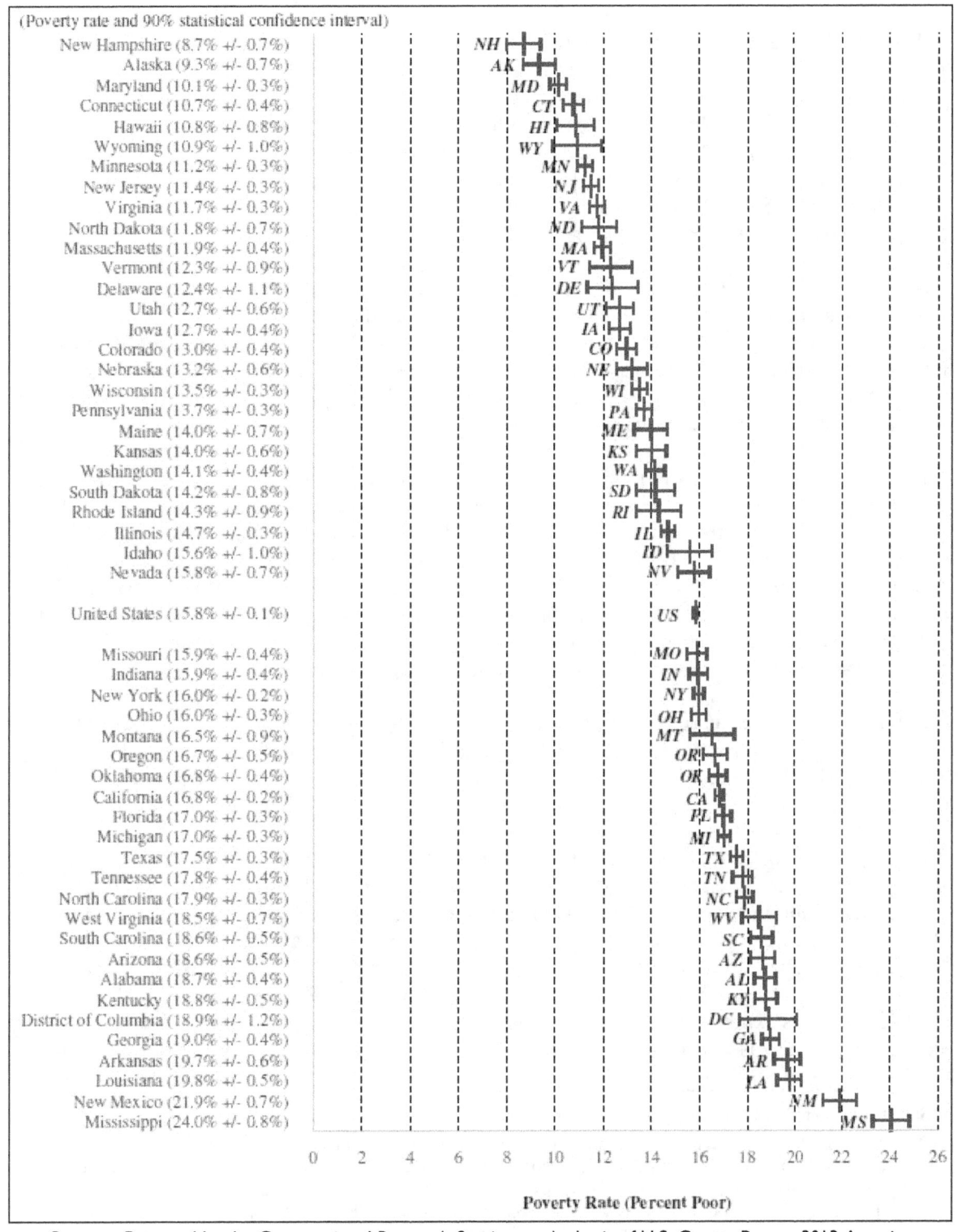

Source: Prepared by the Congressional Research Service on the basis of U.S. Census Bureau 2013 American Community Survey (ACS) data.

Change in State Poverty Rates: 2002-2013

Table 1 provides estimates of state and national poverty rates from 2002 through 2013 from the ACS. Statistically significant changes from one year to the next are indicated by an upward-pointing arrow (▲) if a state's poverty rate was statistically higher, and by a downward-pointing arrow (▼) if statistically lower, than in the immediately preceding year or for other selected periods (i.e., 2005 vs. 2002, 2013 vs. 2007).[14] It should be noted that ACS poverty estimates for 2006 and later are not strictly comparable to those of earlier years, due to a change in ACS methodology that began in 2006 to include some persons living in non-institutionalized group quarters who were not included in earlier years.[15]

Table 1 shows that three states (New Jersey, New Mexico, and Washington) experienced statistically significant increases in their poverty rates from the 2012 to 2013 ACS. New Jersey's estimated poverty rate increased from 10.8% in 2012, to11.4% in 2013, while New Mexico's rate increased from 20.8% to 21.9%, and Washington's rate increased from 13.5% to 14.1%, over the period. Four states (Colorado, New Hampshire, Texas, and Wyoming) experienced statistically significant decreases in their poverty rates from 2012 to 2013.

The table shows that poverty among states generally increased over the 2002 to 2005 period, as measured by the ACS, consequent to the 2001 (March to November) economic recession. From the 2002 to 2003 ACS, five states (including the District of Columbia) experienced statistically significant increases in their poverty rates, whereas none experienced a statistically significant decrease. From 2003 to 2004, eight states saw their poverty rates increase, whereas two saw decreases. From 2004 to 2005, 13 states saw their poverty rates increase, whereas only 1 saw its poverty rate decrease. Comparing poverty rates from the 2005 ACS to those from the 2002 ACS, poverty was statistically higher in 22 states, and lower in only one.

By 2007, poverty rates among states were beginning to improve, with 13 states (including the District of Columbia) experiencing statistically significant declines in their poverty rates from 2006; only Michigan experienced a statistically significant increase in its poverty rate in 2007 compared to a year earlier.

Since 2007, state poverty rates have generally increased consequent to the 18-month recession (December 2007 to June 2009). From 2007 to 2008, the ACS data showed eight states (California, Connecticut, Florida, Hawaii, Indiana, Michigan, Oregon, and Pennsylvania) as experiencing statistically significant increases in their poverty rates, whereas three states (Alabama, Louisiana, and Texas) experienced statistically significant decreases. From 2008 to 2009, 32 states saw their poverty rates increase, and no state experienced a statistically significant decrease, and from 2009 to 2010, 34 states experienced statistically significant increases in poverty, and again, no state experienced a decrease. As noted above, from 2012 to 2013, three states saw their poverty rates

---

[14] Statistically significant differences are based on a 90% statistical confidence interval.

[15] Beginning in 2006, a portion of the population living in non-institutional group quarters has been included in the ACS in estimating poverty. The population living in institutional group quarters, military barracks, and college dormitories has been excluded in the ACS poverty estimates for all years. The part of the non-institutional group quarters population that has been included in the poverty universe since 2006 (e.g., people living in group homes or those living in agriculture workers' dormitories) is considerably more likely to be in poverty than people living in households. Consequently, estimates of poverty in 2006 and after are somewhat higher than would be the case if all group quarters residents were excluded—thus, comparisons with earlier year estimates are not strictly comparable.

rise, and four saw a decline. Comparing 2013 to 2007, poverty rates were statistically higher in 48 states (including the District of Columbia), and no state had a poverty rate statistically below its prerecession rate.

Table 1. Poverty Rates for the 50 States and the District of Columbia, 2002 to 2013 Estimates from the American Community Survey (ACS)

(percent poor)

	Estimated Poverty Rates and Statistically Significant Differences over Previous Year												Change in Poverty Rates over Selected Periods and Statistically Significant Differences[a]	
	2002	2003	2004	2005	2006[b]	2007[b]	2008[b]	2009[b]	2010[b]	2011[b]	2012[b]	2013[b]	2005 vs. 2001	2013 vs. 2007
United States	12.4	12.7	13.1	13.3	13.3	13.0	13.2	14.3	15.3	15.9	15.9	15.8	0.9	2.9
Alabama	16.6	17.1	16.1	17.0	16.6	16.9	15.7	17.5	19.0	19.0	19.0	18.7	0.4	1.9
Alaska	7.7	9.7	8.2	11.2	10.9	8.9	8.4	9.0	9.9	10.5	10.1	9.3	3.5	0.4
Arizona	14.2	15.4	14.2	14.2	14.2	14.2	14.7	16.5	17.4	19.0	18.7	18.6	0.0	4.5
Arkansas	15.3	16.0	17.9	17.2	17.3	17.9	17.3	18.8	18.8	19.5	19.8	19.7	1.9	1.8
California	13.0	13.4	13.3	13.3	13.1	12.4	13.3	14.2	15.8	16.6	17.0	16.8	0.3	4.4
Colorado	9.7	9.8	11.1	11.1	12.0	12.0	11.4	12.9	13.4	13.5	13.7	13.0	1.4	1.0
Connecticut	7.5	8.1	7.6	8.3	8.3	7.9	9.3	9.4	10.1	10.9	10.7	10.7	0.9	2.8
Delaware	8.2	8.7	9.9	10.4	11.1	10.5	10.0	10.8	11.8	11.9	12.0	12.4	2.2	1.9
Dist. of Col.	17.5	19.9	18.9	19.0	19.6	16.4	17.2	18.4	19.2	18.7	18.2	18.9	1.6	2.5
Florida	12.8	13.1	12.2	12.8	12.6	12.1	13.2	14.9	16.5	17.0	17.1	17.0	0.0	4.9
Georgia	12.7	13.4	14.8	14.4	14.7	14.3	14.7	16.5	17.9	19.1	19.2	19.0	1.7	4.7
Hawaii	10.1	10.9	10.6	9.8	9.3	8.0	9.1	10.4	10.7	12.0	11.6	10.8	-0.3	2.9
Idaho	13.8	13.8	14.5	13.9	12.6	12.1	12.6	14.3	15.7	16.5	15.9	15.6	0.0	3.4
Illinois	11.6	11.3	11.9	12.0	12.3	11.9	12.2	13.3	13.8	15.0	14.7	14.7	0.4	2.7
Indiana	10.9	10.6	10.8	12.2	12.7	12.3	13.1	14.4	15.3	16.0	15.6	15.9	1.3	3.6
Iowa	11.2	10.1	9.9	10.9	11.0	11.0	11.5	11.8	12.6	12.8	12.7	12.7	-0.3	1.6
Kansas	12.1	10.8	10.5	11.7	12.4	11.2	11.3	13.4	13.6	13.8	14.0	14.0	-0.4	2.8

Estimated Poverty Rates and Statistically Significant Differences over Previous Year

	2002	2003	2004	2005	2006[b]	2007[b]	2008[b]	2009[b]	2010[b]	2011[b]	2012[b]	2013[b]	Change in Poverty Rates over Selected Periods and Statistically Significant Differences[a] 2005 vs. 2001	2013 vs. 2007
Kentucky	15.6	17.4	17.4	16.8	17.0	17.3	17.3	18.6	19.0	19.1	19.4	18.8	1.2	1.4
Louisiana	18.8	20.3	19.4	19.8	19.0	18.6	17.3	17.3	18.7	20.4	19.9	19.8	1.0	1.1
Maine	11.1	10.5	12.3	12.6	12.9	12.0	12.3	12.3	12.9	14.1	14.7	14.0	1.5	1.9
Maryland	8.1	8.2	8.8	8.2	7.8	8.3	8.1	9.1	9.9	10.1	10.3	10.1	0.2	1.8
Massachusetts	8.9	9.4	9.2	10.3	9.9	9.9	10.0	10.3	11.4	11.6	11.9	11.9	1.4	2.0
Michigan	11.0	11.4	12.3	13.2	13.5	14.0	14.4	16.2	16.8	17.5	17.4	17.0	2.2	3.0
Minnesota	8.5	7.8	8.3	9.2	9.8	9.5	9.6	11.0	11.6	11.9	11.4	11.2	0.6	1.7
Mississippi	19.9	19.9	21.6	21.3	21.1	20.6	21.2	21.9	22.4	22.6	24.2	24.0	1.5	3.4
Missouri	11.9	11.7	11.8	13.3	13.6	13.0	13.4	14.6	15.3	15.8	16.2	15.9	1.4	2.9
Montana	14.6	14.2	14.2	14.4	13.6	14.1	14.8	15.1	14.6	14.8	15.5	16.5	-0.3	2.4
Nebraska	11.0	10.8	11.0	10.9	11.5	11.2	10.8	12.3	12.9	13.1	13.0	13.2	0.0	2.0
Nevada	11.8	11.5	12.6	11.1	10.3	10.7	11.3	12.4	14.9	15.9	16.4	15.8	-0.7	5.1
New Hampshire	6.4	7.7	7.6	7.5	8.0	7.1	7.6	8.5	8.3	8.8	10.0	8.7	1.1	1.6
New Jersey	7.5	8.4	8.5	8.7	8.7	8.6	8.7	9.4	10.3	10.4	10.8	11.4	1.2	2.9
New Mexico	18.9	18.6	19.3	18.5	18.5	18.1	17.1	18.0	20.4	21.5	20.8	21.9	-0.4	3.8
New York	13.1	13.5	14.2	13.8	14.2	13.7	13.6	14.2	14.9	16.0	15.9	16.0	0.7	2.3
North Carolina	14.2	14.0	15.2	15.1	14.7	14.3	14.6	16.3	17.5	17.9	18.0	17.9	0.8	3.6
North Dakota	12.5	11.7	12.1	11.2	11.4	12.1	12.0	11.7	13.0	12.2	11.2	11.8	-1.3	-0.3
Ohio	11.9	12.1	12.5	13.0	13.3	13.1	13.4	15.2	15.8	16.4	16.3	16.0	1.2	2.8
Oklahoma	15.0	16.1	15.3	16.5	17.0	15.9	15.9	16.2	16.9	17.2	17.2	16.8	1.5	0.9
Oregon	13.2	13.9	14.1	14.1	13.3	12.9	13.6	14.3	15.8	17.5	17.2	16.7	0.9	3.7

Estimated Poverty Rates and Statistically Significant Differences over Previous Year

	2002	2003	2004	2005	2006[b]	2007[b]	2008[b]	2009[b]	2010[b]	2011[b]	2012[b]	2013[b]	2005 vs. 2001	2013 vs. 2007
Pennsylvania	10.5	10.9	11.7	11.9	12.1	11.6	12.1	12.5	13.4	13.8	13.7	13.7	1.4	2.1
Rhode Island	10.7	11.3	12.8	12.3	11.1	12.0	11.7	11.5	14.0	14.7	13.7	14.3	1.6	2.3
South Carolina	14.2	14.1	15.7	15.6	15.7	15.0	15.7	17.1	18.2	18.9	18.3	18.6	1.3	3.5
South Dakota	11.4	11.1	11.0	13.6	13.6	13.1	12.5	14.2	14.4	13.9	13.4	14.2	2.3	1.1
Tennessee	14.5	13.8	14.5	15.5	16.2	15.9	15.5	17.1	17.7	18.3	17.9	17.8	1.0	1.9
Texas	15.6	16.3	16.6	17.6	16.9	16.3	15.8	17.2	17.9	18.5	17.9	17.5	2.0	1.3
Utah	10.5	10.6	10.9	10.2	10.6	9.7	9.6	11.5	13.2	13.5	12.8	12.7	-0.3	3.0
Vermont	8.5	9.7	9.0	11.5	10.3	10.1	10.6	11.4	12.7	11.5	11.8	12.3	2.9	2.2
Virginia	9.9	9.0	9.5	10.0	9.6	9.9	10.2	10.5	11.1	11.5	11.7	11.7	0.0	1.8
Washington	11.4	11.0	13.1	11.9	11.8	11.4	11.3	12.3	13.4	13.9	13.5	14.1	0.5	2.7
West Virginia	17.2	18.5	17.9	18.0	17.3	16.9	17.0	17.7	18.1	18.6	17.8	18.5	0.8	1.6
Wisconsin	9.7	10.5	10.7	10.2	11.0	10.8	10.4	12.4	13.2	13.1	13.2	13.5	0.5	2.7
Wyoming	11.0	9.7	10.3	9.5	9.4	8.7	9.4	9.8	11.2	11.3	12.6	10.9	-1.5	2.2
Number of states with statistically significant change in poverty:		5	10	14	7	14	11	32	34	18	5	7	23	48
Increase in poverty		5	8	13	4	1	8	32	34	17	3	3	22	48
Decrease in poverty		0	2	1	3	13	3	0	0	1	2	4	1	0

Source: Congressional Research Service (CRS) estimates from U.S. Census Bureau American Community Survey (ACS) data, 2002 to 2013.

Notes: ▲ Statistically significant increase in poverty rate at the 90% statistical confidence level.

▼ Statistically significant decrease in poverty rate at the 90% statistical confidence level.

a. Depicted changes in poverty rates over selected periods may differ slightly from differences calculated directly from the table, due to rounding.

b. Comparisons to 2002 through 2005 estimates are not strictly comparable, due to inclusion of persons living in some non-institutional group quarters beginning in 2006 and after.

Poverty Rates by Metropolitan Area

The four tables that follow provide poverty estimates for large metropolitan areas having a population of 500,000 and over, and for smaller metropolitan areas having a population of 50,000 or more but less than 500,000. Among large metropolitan areas, 10 areas with some of the lowest poverty rates are shown in **Table 2**, and the 10 areas with some of the highest poverty rates are shown in **Table 3**. Among smaller metropolitan areas, 10 areas with some of the lowest poverty rates are shown in **Table 4**, and 10 among those with the highest poverty rates in **Table 5**. It should be noted that metropolitan areas shown in these tables may not be statistically different from one another, or from others not shown in the tables. Poverty estimates for all metropolitan areas in 2013 are shown in **Appendix B. Table B-1**.

Table 2. Large Metropolitan Areas Among Those with the Lowest Poverty Rates: 2013

(Metropolitan Areas with Population of 500,000 and Over)

Metropolitan Area	Total Population	Number Poor		Poverty Rate (Percent Poor)	
		Estimate	Margin of Error[a]	Estimate	Margin of Error[a]
Washington-Arlington-Alexandria, DC-VA-MD-WV	5,846,655	495,683	+/-19,944	8.5%	+/-0.3%
Urban Honolulu, HI	951,718	89,684	+/-7,816	9.4%	+/-0.8%
Bridgeport-Stamford-Norwalk, CT	921,302	88,808	+/-6,895	9.6%	+/-0.7%
Minneapolis-St. Paul-Bloomington, MN-WI	3,397,278	349,161	+/-13,880	10.3%	+/-0.4%
Boston-Cambridge-Newton, MA-NH	4,525,102	470,178	+/-18,981	10.4%	+/-0.4%
Lancaster, PA	514,196	53,694	+/-5,804	10.4%	+/-1.1%
Ogden-Clearfield, UT	615,823	64,161	+/-7,360	10.4%	+/-1.2%
San Jose-Sunnyvale-Santa Clara, CA	1,891,182	198,842	+/-12,625	10.5%	+/-0.7%
Colorado Springs, CO	660,782	71,297	+/-7,162	10.8%	+/-1.1%
Hartford-West Hartford-East Hartford, CT	1,169,485	125,923	+/-9,009	10.8%	+/-0.8%

Source: Table prepared by the Congressional Research Service (CRS) based on analysis of U.S. Census Bureau 2012 American Community Survey (ACS) data, table series S1701: Poverty Status in the Past 12 Months, from the Census Bureau's American FactFinder, available at http://factfinder2.census.gov/faces/nav/jsf/pages/index.xhtml.

Notes: Areas are included based on their estimated 2013 poverty rates. Areas shown may not be statistically different from one another, or from others not shown in the table.

a. Margin of error of an estimate based on a 90% statistical confidence level. When added to and subtracted from an estimate, the range reflects a 90% statistical confidence interval bounding the estimate.

Table 3. Large Metropolitan Areas Among Those with the Highest Poverty Rates: 2013

(Metropolitan Areas with Population of 500,000 and Over)

Metropolitan Area	Total Population	Number Poor		Poverty Rate (Percent Poor)	
		Estimate	Margin of Error[a]	Estimate	Margin of Error[a]
McAllen-Edinburg-Mission, TX	803,934	275,681	+/-16,441	34.3%	+/-2.0%
Fresno, CA	937,990	270,072	+/-12,767	28.8%	+/-1.4%
Bakersfield, CA	831,344	189,484	+/-13,393	22.8%	+/-1.6%
El Paso, TX	816,158	184,427	+/-12,589	22.6%	+/-1.5%
Modesto, CA	518,152	114,628	+/-9,386	22.1%	+/-1.8%
Jackson, MS	557,607	122,754	+/-7,806	22.0%	+/-1.4%
Winston-Salem, NC	636,242	127,378	+/-10,165	20.0%	+/-1.6%
Greensboro-High Point, NC	722,405	143,646	+/-9,658	19.9%	+/-1.3%
Stockton-Lodi, CA	690,366	137,663	+/-9,607	19.9%	+/-1.4%
Augusta-Richmond County, GA-SC	565,819	111,863	+/-8,976	19.8%	+/-1.6%

Source: Table prepared by the Congressional Research Service (CRS) based on analysis of U.S. Census Bureau 2012 American Community Survey (ACS) data, table series S1701: Poverty Status in the Past 12 Months, from the Census Bureau's American FactFinder, available at http://factfinder2.census.gov/faces/nav/jsf/pages/index.xhtml.

Notes: Areas are included based on their estimated 2013 poverty rates. Areas shown may not be statistically different from one another, or from others not shown in the table.

a.   Margin of error of an estimate based on a 90% statistical confidence level. When added to and subtracted from an estimate, the range reflects a 90% statistical confidence interval bounding the estimate.

Table 4. Smaller Metropolitan Areas Among Those with the Lowest Poverty Rates: 2013

(Metropolitan Areas with Populations Between 50,000 and 499,999)

Metropolitan Area	Total Population	Number Poor		Poverty Rate (Percent Poor)	
		Estimate	Margin of Error[a]	Estimate	Margin of Error[a]
California-Lexington Park, MD	106,530	6,831	+/-2,204	6.4%	+/-2.1%
Winchester, VA-WV	124,642	8,432	+/-1,934	6.8%	+/-1.5%
Anchorage, AK	386,833	27,596	+/-3,586	7.1%	+/-0.9%
Fairbanks, AK	96,578	7,442	+/-2,543	7.7%	+/-2.6%
Rochester, MN	208,650	16,523	+/-2,572	7.9%	+/-1.2%
Appleton, WI	226,221	18,291	+/-2,940	8.1%	+/-1.3%
Fond du Lac, WI	98,663	8,023	+/-1,707	8.1%	+/-1.7%

Bismarck, ND	121,277	10,119	+/-1,758	8.3%	+/-1.5%
Gettysburg, PA	97,009	8,620	+/-2,132	8.9%	+/-2.2%
Napa, CA	136,394	12,286	+/-2,875	9.0%	+/-2.1%

Source: Table prepared by the Congressional Research Service (CRS) based on analysis of U.S. Census Bureau 2012 American Community Survey (ACS) data, table series S1701: Poverty Status in the Past 12 Months, from the Census Bureau's American FactFinder, available at http://factfinder2.census.gov/faces/nav/jsf/pages/index.xhtml.

Notes: Areas are included based on their estimated 2013 poverty rates. Areas shown may not be statistically different from one another, or from others not shown in the table.

a. Margin of error of an estimate based on a 90% statistical confidence level. When added to and subtracted from an estimate, the range reflects a 90% statistical confidence interval bounding the estimate.

Table 5. Smaller Metropolitan Areas Among Those with the Highest Poverty Rates: 2013

(Metropolitan Areas with Population of 500,000 and Over)

Metropolitan Area	Total Population	Number Poor		Poverty Rate (Percent Poor)	
		Estimate	Margin of Error[a]	Estimate	Margin of Error[a]
Brownsville-Harlingen, TX	412,432	134,170	+/-8,943	32.5%	+/-2.2%
Laredo, TX	258,684	80,403	+/-7,285	31.1%	+/-2.8%
Visalia-Porterville, CA	448,360	135,066	+/-9,722	30.1%	+/-2.2%
Athens-Clarke County, GA	186,981	53,388	+/-5,015	28.6%	+/-2.6%
College Station-Bryan, TX	224,477	63,800	+/-6,284	28.4%	+/-2.8%
Las Cruces, NM	208,101	57,908	+/-6,390	27.8%	+/-3.1%
Valdosta, GA	139,018	37,443	+/-4,673	26.9%	+/-3.3%
Gainesville, FL	256,894	68,758	+/-5,496	26.8%	+/-2.1%
Greenville, NC	168,611	43,223	+/-5,197	25.6%	+/-3.1%
Monroe, LA	168,802	42,735	+/-5,063	25.3%	+/-3.0%

Source: Table prepared by the Congressional Research Service (CRS) based on analysis of U.S. Census Bureau 2012 American Community Survey (ACS) data, table series S1701: Poverty Status in the Past 12 Months, from the Census Bureau's American FactFinder, available at http://factfinder2.census.gov/faces/nav/jsf/pages/index.xhtml.

Notes: Areas are included based on their estimated 2013 poverty rates. Areas shown may not be statistically different from one another, or from others not shown in the table.

a. Margin of error of an estimate based on a 90% statistical confidence level. When added to and subtracted from an estimate, the range reflects a 90% statistical confidence interval bounding the estimate.

Congressional District Poverty Estimates

Poverty estimates for congressional districts are shown in **Appendix C**. **Table C-1** includes poverty rate estimates for 2012. Congressional districts in 2012 are not directly comparable to earlier years, due to re-districting.

"Neighborhood" Poverty—Poverty Areas and Areas of Concentrated and Extreme Poverty

The estimates presented here are based on five years of American Community Survey (ACS) data (2006-2010 ACS), and will be updated once the Census Bureau releases 5-year ACS estimates for 2008-2012, in December 2014.

Neighborhoods can be delineated from U.S. Census Bureau census tracts. Census tracts usually have between 2,500 and 8,000 persons and, when first delineated, are designed to be homogeneous with respect to population characteristics, economic status, and living conditions. The Census Bureau defines "poverty areas" as census tracts having poverty rates of 20% or more.

Figure 7 groups census tracts according to their level of poverty. The first two groupings are based on poor persons living in census tracts with poverty rates below the national average (13.8% based on the five-year ACS data), and from 13.8% to less than 20.0%. Poor persons living in census tracts with poverty rates of 20% or more meet the Census Bureau definition of living in "poverty areas." Poverty areas are further demarcated in terms of poor persons living in areas of "concentrated" poverty (i.e., census tracts with poverty rates of 30% to 39.9%), and areas of "extreme" poverty (i.e., census tracts with poverty rates of 40% or more). The figure is based on five years of data (2006–2010) from the U.S. Census Bureau's American Community Survey (ACS). Five years of data are required in order to get reasonably reliable statistical data at the census tract level while at the same time preserving the confidentiality of survey respondents.

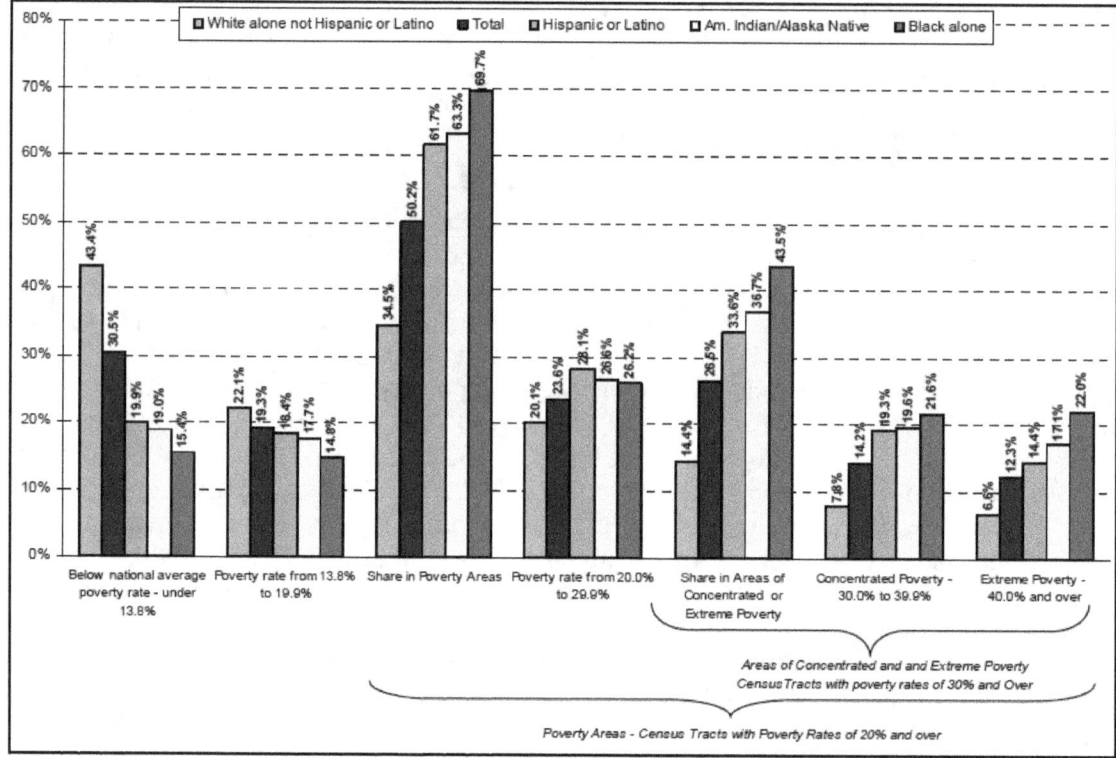

Figure 7. Distribution of Poor People by Race and Hispanic Origin, by Level of Neighborhood (Census Tract) Poverty, 2006-2010

Source: Congressional Research Service (CRS) analysis of U.S. Census Bureau American Community Survey, five-year (2006-2010) data.

Figure 7 shows that over the five-year period 2006–2010, half of all poor persons (50.2%) lived in "poverty areas" (i.e., census tracts with poverty rates of 20% or more). Over one-quarter (26.5%) lived in areas with poverty of 30% or more, and about one in eight (12.3%) lived in areas of "extreme" poverty, having poverty rates of 40% or more. Among the poor, African Americans, American Indian and Alaska Natives, and Hispanics are more likely to live in poverty areas than either Asians or white non-Hispanics. Among poor blacks, over two of every five (43.5%) live in neighborhoods with poverty rates of 30% or more, and over one in five (22.0%) live in "extreme" poverty areas, with poverty rates of 40% or more. Among Hispanics, one-third (33.6%) live in areas with poverty rates of 30% or more, and about one in seven (14.4%) live in areas of "extreme" poverty. Among white non-Hispanics, close to two-thirds (64.5%) live outside poverty areas, while about one in seven (14.4%) live in areas with poverty rates of 30% or more.

The Research Supplemental Poverty Measure

The estimates presented here are based on 2012 Census Bureau Supplemental Poverty Measure Estimates. This section will be updated once the Census Bureau issues 2013 Supplemental Poverty Measure estimates in late-October 2014.

On November 6, 2013, the Census Bureau released its third annual report using a new Supplemental Poverty Measure (SPM).[16] As its name implies, the SPM is intended to "supplement," rather than replace, the "official" poverty measure. The "official" Census Bureau statistical measure of poverty will continue to be used by programs that allocate funds to states or other jurisdictions on the basis of poverty, and the Department of Health and Human Services (HHS) will continue to derive Poverty Income Guidelines from the "official" Census Bureau measure.

Many experts consider the "official" poverty measure to be flawed and outmoded.[17] In 1990, Congress commissioned a study on how poverty is measured in the United States, resulting in the National Academy of Sciences (NAS) convening a 12-member expert panel to study the issue. The NAS panel issued a wide range of specific recommendations to develop an improved statistical measure of poverty in its 1995 report *Measuring Poverty: A New Approach.*[18]

In late 2009, the Office of Management and Budget (OMB) formed an Interagency Technical Working Group[19] (ITWG) to suggest how the Census Bureau, in cooperation with the Bureau of Labor Statistics (BLS), should develop a new Supplemental Poverty Measure, using the NAS expert panel's recommendations as a starting point. Referencing the work of the ITWG,[20] the Department of Commerce announced in March 2010 that the Census Bureau was developing a new Supplemental Poverty Measure, as "an alternative lens to understand poverty and measure the effects of anti-poverty policies," with the intention that the new measure "will be dynamic and will benefit from improvements over time based on new data and new methodologies."[21]

The SPM is intended to address a number of weaknesses of the "official" measure. Criticisms of the "official" poverty measure raised by the NAS expert panel include the following:

- *The "official" poverty measure, by counting only families' total cash, pre-tax income as a resource in determining poverty status, ignores a host of government programs and policies that affect the disposable income families may actually have available.* For example, the official measure ignores the effects of payroll taxes paid by families, and tax benefits they may receive such as the EITC and the Child Tax Credit. It ignores a variety of in-kind benefits, such as SNAP benefits and free or reduced-price lunches under the National School Lunch Program, that free up resources to meet other needs. Similarly, it ignores housing subsidies that help make housing more affordable.

---

[16] Kathleen Short, *The Research SUPPLEMENTAL POVERTY MEASURE: 2011*, U.S. Census Bureau, P60-244, Washington, DC, November 2012, http://www.census.gov/prod/2012pubs/p60-244.pdf.

[17] For a discussion of the history and development of the U.S. poverty measure, and efforts to improve poverty measurement, see CRS Report R41187, *Poverty Measurement in the United States: History, Current Practice, and Proposed Changes*, by Thomas Gabe.

[18] National Research Council, Panel on Poverty and Family Assistance, "Measuring Poverty: A New Approach," Constance F. Citro and Robert T. Michael, eds. (Washington, DC: National Academy Press, 1995). (Hereinafter cited as Citro and Michael, *Measuring Poverty...*)

[19] The working group included representatives from BLS, the Census Bureau, the Council of Economic Advisors, the Department of Commerce, the Department of Health and Human Services, and OMB.

[20] The ITWG's guidance is available at http://www.census.gov/hhes/www/poverty/SPM_TWGObservations.pdf

[21] *Census Bureau to Develop Supplemental Poverty Measure*, March 2, 2010 News Release, Economics and Statistics Administration, U.S. Department of Commerce. Available on the Internet at http://www.esa.doc.gov/news/2010/03/02/census-bureau-develop-supplemental-poverty-measure.

- *The "official" poverty income thresholds used in determining families' and individuals' poverty status, devised in the early 1960s, have changed little since.* Except for minor technical changes and adjustments for price inflation, poverty income thresholds have essentially been frozen in time, reflecting living standards of a half-century ago.

- *The "official" poverty measure does not take into account necessary work-related expenses, such as child care and transportation costs that are associated with getting to work.* Child care expenses are much more common today than when the "official" poverty measure was originally developed, as mothers' labor force participation has since increased.

- *The "official" poverty measure does not take into account medical expenses that individuals and families may incur, affecting their ability to meet other basic needs.* These costs, which tend to vary by age, health status, and insurance coverage of individuals, may differentially affect families' abilities to meet other basic needs, especially given rising health care costs.

- *The "official" poverty measure does not take into account changing family situations, such as cohabitation among unmarried couples, or child support payments.*

- *The "official" poverty measure does not adjust for differences in prices across geographic areas, which may affect the cost of living from one area to another.*

The ITWG, using the NAS-panel recommendations as a starting point, suggested an approach to developing the SPM that addressed how income thresholds should be set and resources counted in measuring poverty. Conceptual differences between the "official" and supplemental poverty measures are summarized in **Table 6**.

Table 6. Poverty Measure Concepts Under "Official" and Supplemental Measures

	"Official" Poverty Measure	Supplemental Poverty Measure
Measurement units	Families and unrelated individuals	All related individuals who live at the same address, including any co-resident unrelated children who are cared for by the family (such as foster children) and any cohabitors and their children

	"Official" Poverty Measure	**Supplemental Poverty Measure**
Poverty threshold	Three times the cost of a minimum food diet in 1963	A range around the 33rd percentile (i.e., 30th to 36th percentile) of expenditures on food, shelter, clothing, and utilities (FCSU) for consumer units with exactly two children multiplied by 1.2 to account for other family needs (e.g., household supplies, personal care, non-transportation-related expenses)
		Based on data from the U.S. Bureau of Labor Statistics Consumer Expenditure Survey (BLS CE)
		Separate thresholds developed for - homeowners with a mortgage, - homeowners without a mortgage, - renters
Threshold adjustments	Vary by family size, composition, and age of householder	A three parameter equivalence scale for number of adults and children in the family
		Geographic adjustments for differences in housing costs
Updating thresholds	Consumer Price Index for Urban Consumers (CPI-U) based on all items	Five-year moving average of expenditures on FCSU from the BLS CE

	"Official" Poverty Measure	Supplemental Poverty Measure
Resource measures	Gross before-tax cash income	Sum of cash income **Plus** in-kind benefits that families can use to meet their FCSU needs: • Supplemental Nutritional Assistance (SNAP) • National School Lunch Program • Supplementary Nutrition Program for Women, Infants, and Children (WIC) • Housing Subsidies • Low-Income Home Energy Assistance (LIHEAP) **Plus** refundable tax credits: • Earned Income Tax Credit (EITC) • Refundable portion of the Child Tax Credit (CTC), known as the Additional Child Tax Credit (ACTC) **Minus** nondiscretionary expenses: • federal and state income taxes • payroll taxes • work-related expenses, including work-related child care expenses • medical out-of-pocket expenses (MOOP), including insurance premiums paid • child support paid

Source: Congressional Research Service (CRS). Adapted from Kathleen Short, The *Research SUPPLEMENTAL POVERTY MEASURE: 2011*, U.S. Census Bureau, P60-244, Washington, DC, November 2012, http://www.census.gov/prod/2012pubs/p60-244.pdf.

The SPM incorporates a more comprehensive income/resource definition than that used by the "official" poverty measure, including in-kind benefits (e.g., SNAP) and refundable tax credits (e.g., EITC). It also expands upon the traditional family definition based on blood, marriage, and adoption to include cohabiting partners and their family relatives as part of a broader economic unit for assessing poverty status. The SPM subtracts necessary expenses (i.e., taxes, work-related expenses including child-care, child support paid, medical out-of-pocket [MOOP] expenses) from resources to arrive at a measure of an economic unit's disposable income/resources that may be applied to a standard of need based on food, clothing, shelter, and utilities (FCSU), plus "a little bit more" for everything else. The SPM income/resource thresholds are initially set at a range in the distribution (30th to 36th percentile) of what reference families (families with exactly two children) actually spend on FCSU. Separate thresholds are derived for homeowners with a mortgage and those without a mortgage, and for renters. Thresholds are adjusted for price differences in housing costs by geographic area (metropolitan and nonmetropolitan areas in a state). Thresholds for economic units other than initial reference units (i.e., those with exactly two children) are adjusted upwards or downwards for the number of adults and number of children in the unit.

Poverty Thresholds

As described earlier, the "official" U.S. poverty measure measures cash—pre-tax—income against income thresholds that vary by family size and composition. The thresholds were derived from research that showed that the average U.S. family spent one-third of its pre-tax income on food, based on a USDA 1955 Food Consumption Survey. After pricing minimally adequate food plans for families of varying sizes and compositions, poverty thresholds were derived by multiplying the cost of those food plans by a factor of three (i.e., one-third of the thresholds were assumed to address families' food needs, and two-thirds addressed everything else). The thresholds, established in 1963, are adjusted each year for price inflation.

SPM Poverty Thresholds

The SPM poverty thresholds are based on the NAS panel recommendation that thresholds be based on a point in the empirical distribution that "reference" families spend on food, clothing, shelter, and utilities (FCSU). Based on ITWG's suggestions, the Census Bureau derives FCSU thresholds for "reference" units with exactly two children, between the 30th and 36th percentile of what such units spend on FCSU, averaged over five years of survey data from the BLS Consumer Expenditure (CE) Survey.[22] Whereas "official" poverty thresholds are based on initial thresholds adjusted for price changes over time, the SPM thresholds are based on changes in reference consumer units' actual spending on FCSU over time.

Following the ITWG's suggestion, three separate sets of thresholds are established: one set for homeowners with a mortgage, another set for homeowners without a mortgage, and a third set for renters. Following NAS panel recommendations, the ITWG suggested that initial poverty thresholds based on FCSU be multiplied by a factor of 1.2, to account for all other needs (e.g., household supplies, personal care, non-work-related transportation).[23] Additionally, thresholds are adjusted upward and downward based on SPM reference unit size using a three parameter equivalence scale based on the number of adults and children in the unit.

Lastly, the thresholds are adjusted to account for variation in geographic price differences across metropolitan and nonmetropolitan areas, by state, based on differences in median housing costs across areas relative to the nation. The geographic housing cost adjustment is applied to the shelter portion of the FCSU-based thresholds.

Figure 8 depicts poverty threshold levels under the "official" poverty measure and under the Research SPM for a resource unit consisting of two adults and two children. The figure shows that in 2012, the official poverty threshold for a family with two adults and two children was $23,283. In comparison, for a similar family, the SPM poverty threshold for homeowners with a

---

[22] The NAS panel recommended that the reference family for establishing initial thresholds be based on families with two adults and two children. The ITWG suggested that initial thresholds be based on consumer units with exactly two children, as children reside in a variety of family types (such as single parent families, presence of one or more grandparents, and families with cohabiting adult partners). The NAS panel recommended that initial thresholds be established at between 78% and 83% of median expenditures on FCSU of reference families, which empirically ranged between the 30th and 35th percentiles. The ITWG suggested that initial thresholds be set at a range around the 33rd percentile of expenditures on FCSU for the reference consumer units. The ITWC suggested that five years of CE data be used in establishing thresholds to smooth the change in the thresholds from one year to the next.

[23] The 1.2 multiplier applied to FCSU equals the midpoint of the NAS panel's recommended multiplier of between 1.15 and 1.25.

---

mortgage was $25,784, $2,501 (10.7%) *above* the official poverty threshold, and for homeowners without a mortgage, $21,400, or $1,883 (8.1%) *below* the official threshold. The SPM poverty threshold for renters was $25,105 or $1,883 (7.8%), *above* the official measure.

Figure 8. Poverty Thresholds Under the "Official" Measure and the Research Supplemental Poverty Measure for Units with Two Adults and Two Children: 2012

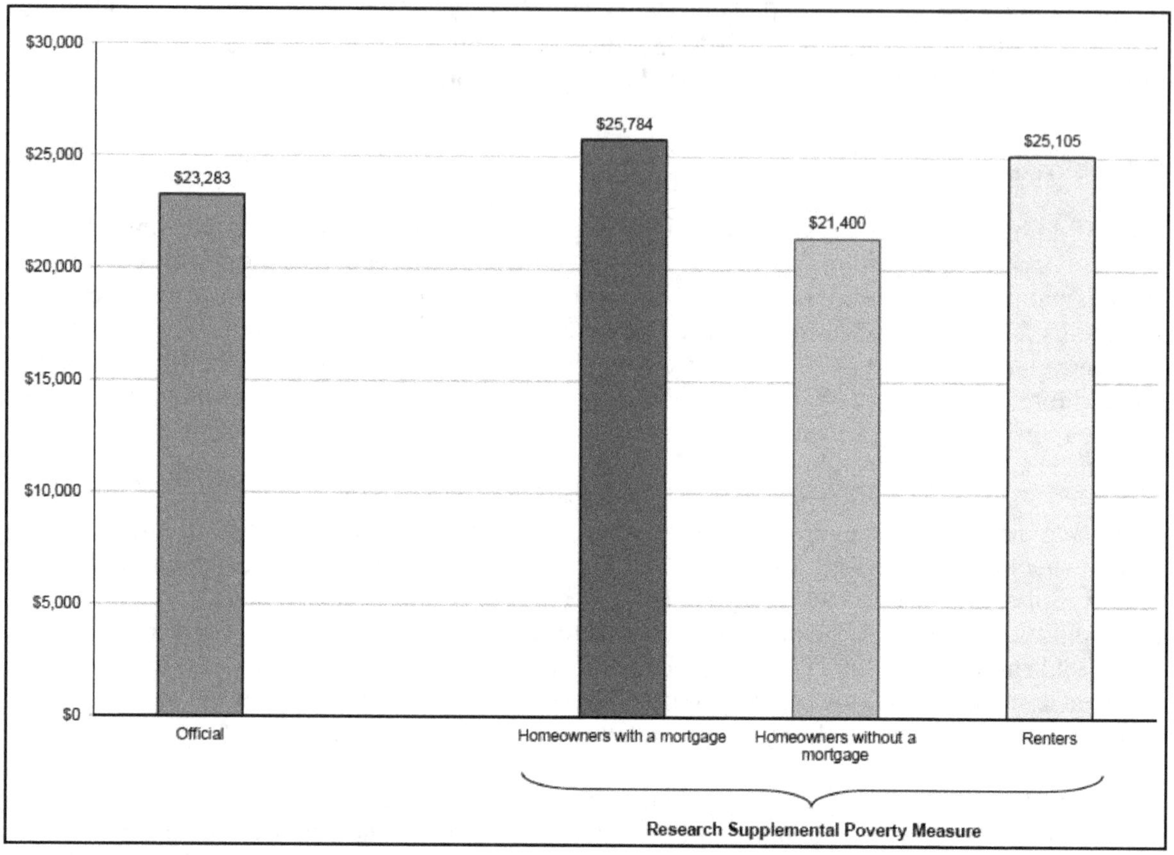

Source: Figure prepared by the Congressional Research Service (CRS), based on Kathleen Short, *The Research SUPPLEMENTAL POVERTY MEASURE: 2012*, U.S. Census Bureau, P60-247, Washington, DC, November 2013 http://www.census.gov/prod/2013pubs/p60-247.pdf.

Resources and Expenses Included in the SPM

As discussed earlier, the "official" poverty measure is based on counting families' and unrelated individuals' pre-tax cash income against poverty thresholds that vary by family size and composition. The SPM expands upon the pre-tax cash income resource definition used by the "official" measure to develop a more comprehensive measure of "disposable" income that SPM units might use to help meet basic needs (i.e., poverty thresholds based on FCSU, plus "a little more"). The SPM resource measure includes the value of a number of federal in-kind benefits, such as Supplemental Nutrition Assistance Program (SNAP, formerly Food Stamp) benefits; free and reduced-price school lunches; nutrition assistance for women, infants, and children (WIC); federal housing assistance; and energy assistance under the Low Income Home Energy Assistance Program (LIHEAP). It also includes federal tax benefits administered by the Internal Revenue

Service, such as the Earned Income Tax Credit (EITC) and the partially refundable portion of the Child Tax Credit (CTC), known as the Additional Child Tax Credit (ACTC).

The SPM subtracts a number of necessary expenses from SPM units' resources to arrive at a measure of "disposable" income that units might have available to meet basic needs. Necessary expenses subtracted from resources on the SPM include child support paid; estimated federal, state, and local income taxes; estimated social security payroll (FICA) taxes; estimated work-related expenses other than child care (e.g., work-related commuting costs, purchase of uniforms or tools required for work); reported work-related child care expenses; and reported medical out of pocket (MOOP) expenses, including the employee share of health insurance premiums plus other medically necessary items such as prescription drugs and doctor copayments.

The effects of counting each of these resources and expenses in the SPM are assessed later in this report (see "Marginal Effects of Counting Specified Resources and Expenses on Poverty Under the SPM").

Poverty Estimates Under the Research SPM Compared to the "Official" Measure

In 2012, the overall poverty rate was somewhat higher under the SPM (16.0%), compared to 15.1% under an "official" poverty measure "adjusted" to include unrelated children typically excluded from the "official" measure.[24] In 2012, an estimated 49.7 million people were poor under the SPM; 2.7 million people more than the 47.0 million estimated under the "official" (adjusted) poverty measure. The remainder of this report focuses on differences in poverty rates among and between various groups under the two measures.

Poverty by Age

The SPM yields a very different impression of the incidence of poverty with respect to age than that portrayed by the "official" measure. **Figure 9** compares poverty rates by age group under the SPM and the "official" measure in 2012. The poverty rate for adults ages 18 to 64 is somewhat higher under the SPM than under the "official" measure (15.5% compared to 13.7%). The figure shows that the poverty rate for children (under age 18) is lower under the SPM than under the "official" measure (18.0% compared to 22.3%). In contrast, the poverty rate among persons age 65 and over is much higher under the SPM than under the "official" measure (14.8% compared to 9.1%). Although the child poverty rate is lower under the SPM than under the "official" measure, and the aged poverty rate is considerably higher, the incidence of poverty among children still exceeds that of the aged under the SPM, as it did under the "official" measure. The SPM paints a much different picture of poverty among the aged than that conveyed by the "official" measure. As will be shown later, much of the difference between the aged poverty rate measured under the SPM compared to the "official" measure is attributable to the effect of medical expenses on the disposable income among aged units to meet basic needs represented by the SPM resource thresholds.

---

[24] "Official" published estimates of poverty exclude unrelated children under the age of 15 in the universe for whom poverty is determined. For comparison with the SPM measure, these children are included in both the "adjusted official" poverty measure and the SPM. Under the "official" published poverty measure, the overall poverty rate was 15.0% in 2012; under the adjusted measure shown in this report, the overall "official" poverty rate in 2012 was 15.1%.

Figure 9. Poverty Rates Under the "Official"* and Research Supplemental Poverty Measures, by Age: 2012

(Percent poor)

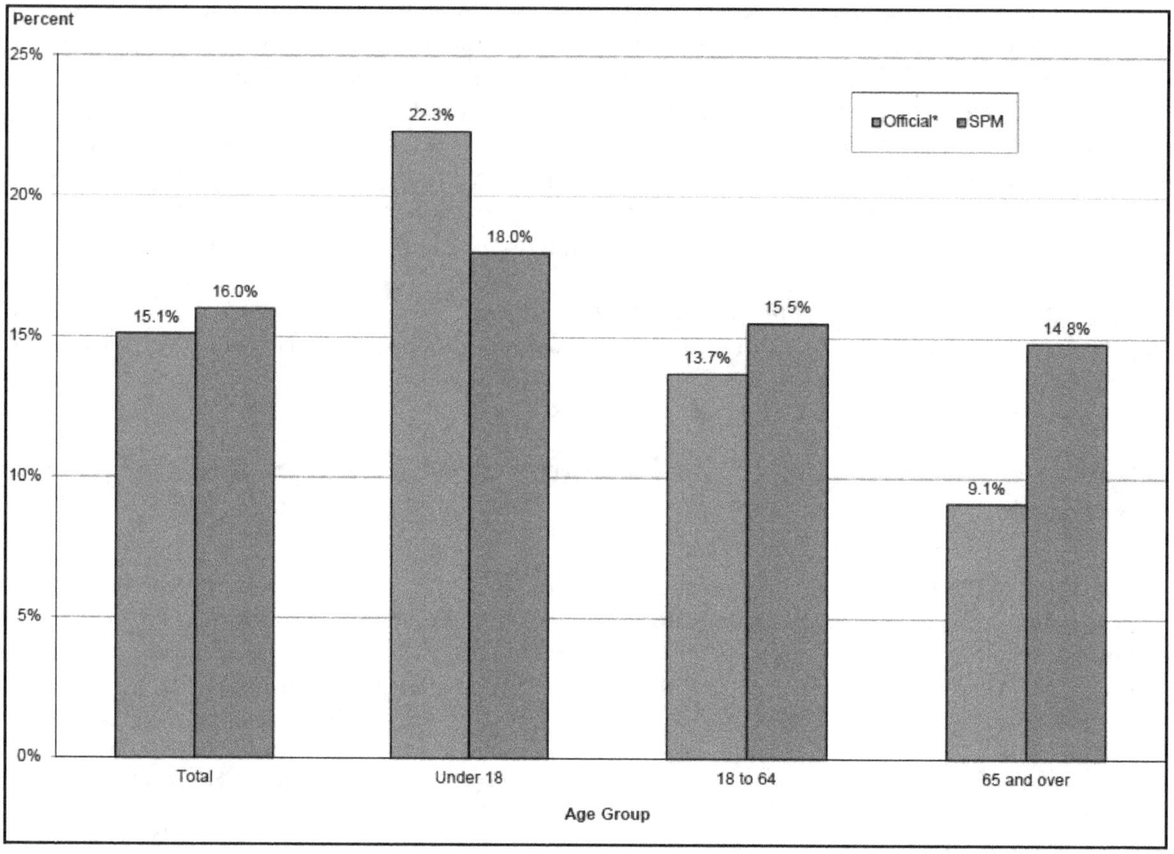

Source: Figure prepared by the Congressional Research Service (CRS), based on Kathleen Short, *The Research SUPPLEMENTAL POVERTY MEASURE: 2012*, U.S. Census Bureau, P60-247, Washington, DC, November 2013 http://www.census.gov/prod/2013pubs/p60-247.pdf.

* Differs from published "official" poverty rates as unrelated individuals under age 15 are included in the universe.

Poverty by Type of Economic Unit

As noted above, the SPM expands the definition of the economic unit considered for poverty measurement purposes over that used under the "official" poverty measure. The "official" poverty measure groups all co-residing household members related by marriage, birth, or adoption as sharing resources for purposes of poverty determination. Unrelated individuals, whether living alone as a single person household or with other unrelated members, are treated as separate economic units under the "official" poverty measure. The "official" measure also excludes unrelated children under age 15 from the universe for poverty determination. As noted earlier, the "adjusted official" poverty measure presented in this section of the report includes unrelated children, resulting in a 15.1% poverty rate as opposed to the published rate of 15.0% in 2012.

The SPM expands the economic unit used for poverty determination beyond that used by the "official" measure.[25] The SPM assesses the relationship of unrelated household members to others in the household to determine whether they will be joined with others to construct expanded economic units. For example, the SPM combines unrelated co-residing household members age 14 and older who are not married and who identify each other as boyfriend, girlfriend, or partner as cohabiting partners. Cohabiting partners, as well as any of their co-resident family members, are combined as an economic unit under the SPM. The SPM also combines unmarried co-residing parents of a child living in the household as an economic unit, even if the parents do not identify as a cohabiting couple. Any unrelated children who are under age 15 and are not foster children are assigned to the householder's economic unit, as are foster children under the age of 22. Additionally, the SPM combines children over age 18 living in a household with a parent, and any younger children of the parent, as an economic unit. Under the "official" poverty measure, a child age 18 and over is treated as an unrelated individual, and the child's parent is also treated as an unrelated individual if no other family members are present, or as an unrelated subfamily head if a spouse or other children (under age 18) are also residing in the household.

In 2012, an estimated 27.9 million persons, 9.0% of the 311.1 million persons represented in the CPS/ASEC, were classified as either joining an economic unit or having members added to their economic unit under the SPM measure, compared to how they would have been classified under the "official" measure's economic unit definition. Combining the resources of these additional household members had the effect of reducing poverty under the SPM measure, compared to the "official" measure, in 2012.

Figure 10 shows poverty rates in 2012 by type of economic unit. Persons identified as being in a married-couple unit, or in female- or male-householder units, are persons in those economic units whose members remained unchanged under the SPM compared to the "official" poverty measure. Persons who were added to an economic unit, or were part of an economic unit that had members added to it under the SPM definition, are labeled as being in a "new SPM unit." The figure shows that poverty rates for persons in married-couple units, and in male-householder units, are higher under the SPM than under the "official" poverty measure (10.0% versus 7.5% for persons in married-couple units, and 23.1% versus 17.9% for persons in male-householder units). Poverty rates for persons living in female-householder units did not statistically differ from one another, with about 3 out of 10 persons in such units considered poor under either measure. In contrast, poverty among persons who were members of "new SPM units" fell by over one-third, from 30.9% under the "official" measure to 18.4% under the SPM.

---

[25] For further discussion, see Ashley J. Provencher, *Unit of Analysis for Poverty Measurement: A Comparison of the Supplemental Poverty Measure and the Official Poverty Measure*, U.S. Census Bureau, SEHSD Working Paper # 2011-22, Washington, DC, August 2, 2011, http://www.census.gov/hhes/povmeas/methodology/supplemental/research/Provencher_JSM.pdf.

Figure 10. Poverty Rates Under the "Official"* and Research Supplemental Poverty Measures, by Type of Economic Unit: 2012

(Percent Poor)

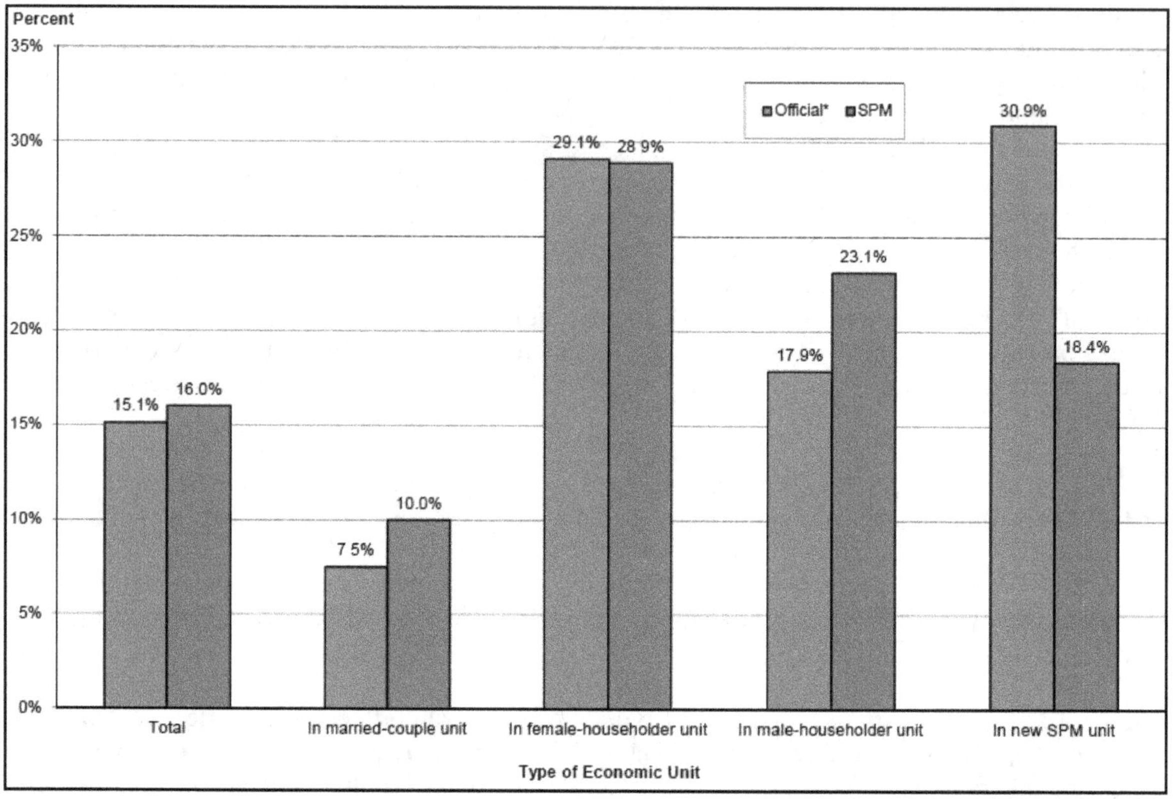

Source: Figure prepared by the Congressional Research Service (CRS), based on Kathleen Short, *The Research SUPPLEMENTAL POVERTY MEASURE: 2012*, U.S. Census Bureau, P60-247, Washington, DC, November 2013 http://www.census.gov/prod/2013pubs/p60-247.pdf.

* Differs from published "official" poverty rates as unrelated individuals under age 15 are included in the universe.

Poverty by Region

Figure 11 compares poverty rates in 2012 under the SPM with the "official" measure by Census region. The figure shows that poverty rates in the West are considerably higher (25% higher) under the SPM (19.0%) than under the "official" measure (15.2%). Poverty rates are about 13% higher in the Northeast under the SPM (15.5%) compared to the "official" measure (13.1%). Poverty rates in the Midwest are lower under the SPM than under the "official" measure, and in the South, essentially equal. The differences in poverty rates within and between regions based on the SPM compared to the "official" measure are most directly due to the SPM's geographic price adjustments to poverty thresholds for differences in the cost of housing in metropolitan and nonmetropolitan areas across states. The cost of housing tends to be higher in the West and Northeast, causing their poverty rates to rise under the SPM relative to the "official" measure and relative to the South and Midwest, where housing tends to be less expensive.

Figure 11. Poverty Rates Under the "Official"* and Research Supplemental Poverty Measures, by Region: 2012

(Percent Poor)

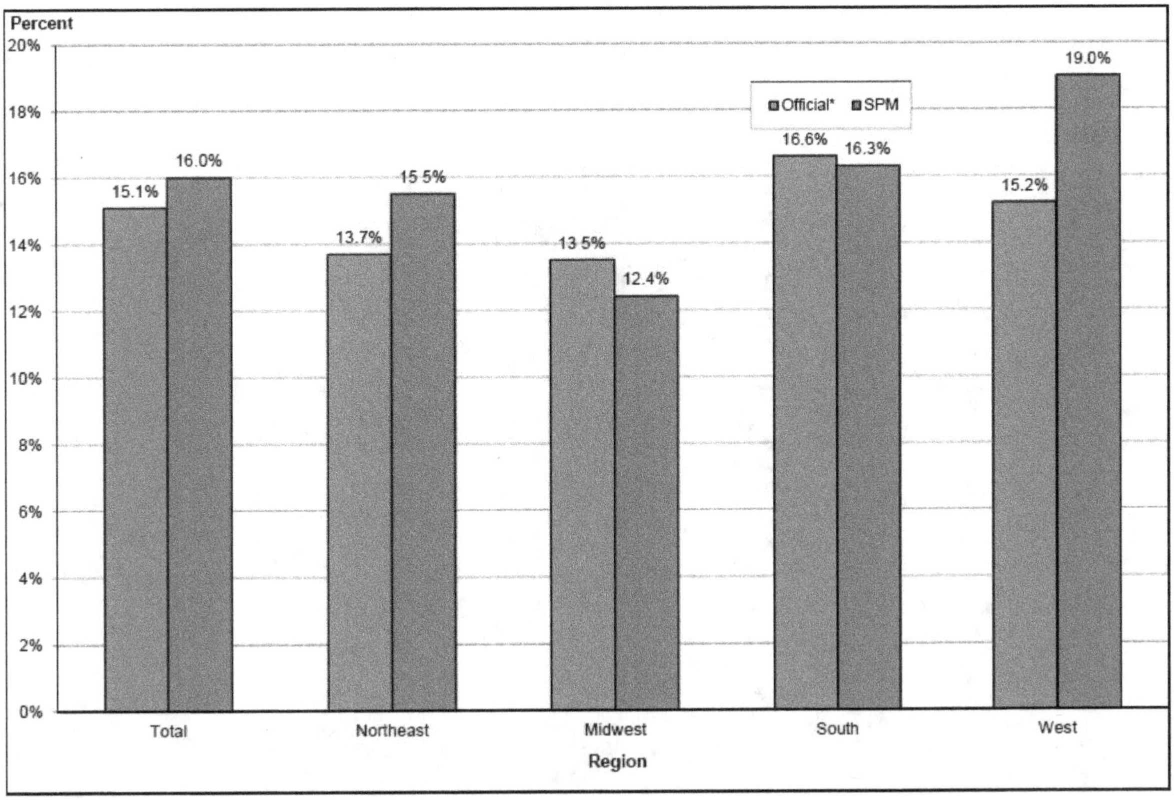

Source: Figure prepared by the Congressional Research Service (CRS), based on Kathleen Short, *The Research SUPPLEMENTAL POVERTY MEASURE: 2012*, U.S. Census Bureau, P60-247, Washington, DC, November 2013 http://www.census.gov/prod/2013pubs/p60-247.pdf.

* Differs from published "official" poverty rates as unrelated individuals under age 15 are included in the universe.

Poverty by Residence

Figure 12 depicts poverty rates by residence in metropolitan (principal city, and outside principal city [i.e., "suburban"]) and nonmetropolitan areas in 2012.[26] The figure shows that under the SPM, the poverty rate for persons living in Metropolitan Statistical Areas (MSAs) (16.4%) is somewhat higher than under the "official" measure (14.6%), whereas for persons living outside MSAs, the poverty rate is lower under the SPM (13.9%) than under the "official" measure (17.9%). Again, this most likely reflects differences in the cost of housing between MSAs and non-MSAs. Within MSAs, poverty rates are higher for persons living within principal cities under both measures than for people living outside them in "suburban" or "ex-urban" areas.

---

[26] The Census Bureau defines Metropolitan Statistical Areas (MSAs) containing a core urban area with a population of 50,000 or more, consisting of one or more counties, that includes the counties containing the urban core area as well as any adjacent counties that have a high degree of social and economic integration (as measured by commuting to work) with the urban core. See http://www.census.gov/population/metro/.

Figure 12. Poverty Rates Under the "Official"* and Research Supplemental Poverty Measures, by Residence: 2012

(Percent Poor)

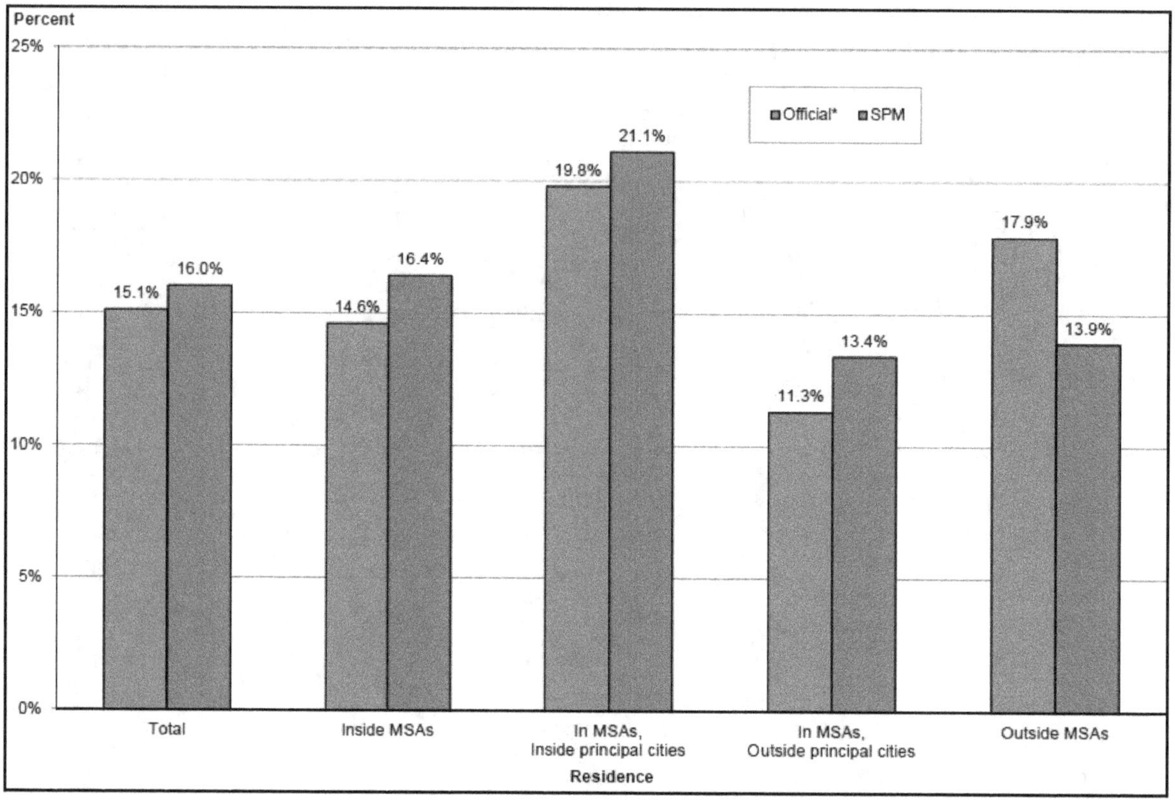

Source: Figure prepared by the Congressional Research Service (CRS), based on Kathleen Short, *The Research SUPPLEMENTAL POVERTY MEASURE: 2012*, U.S. Census Bureau, P60-247, Washington, DC, November 2013 http://www.census.gov/prod/2013pubs/p60-247.pdf.

* Differs from published "official" poverty rates as unrelated individuals under age 15 are included in the universe.

Poverty by State

Figure 13 depicts states according to whether the state's SPM poverty rate statistically differs from its "official" poverty rate.[27] Estimates are based on three-year (2010 to 2012) averages of CPS/ASEC data. Three years of data are combined in order to improve the statistical reliability of CPS/ASEC estimates at the state level. The figure shows that 13 states (California, Colorado, Connecticut, Florida, Hawaii, Illinois, Maryland, Massachusetts, New Hampshire, New Jersey, New York, Nevada, and Virginia) and the District of Columbia had higher poverty rates under the SPM than under the "official" measure. Among the 13 states with higher SPM poverty rates than their respective "official" poverty rate, only Colorado, Illinois, and Nevada were inland, and with the exception of Florida and Virginia, none were in the South. The figure shows that the SPM poverty rate was not statistically different than the "official" poverty rate in nine states (Alaska, Arizona, Delaware, Georgia, Oregon, Pennsylvania, Rhode Island, Utah, and Washington). Among the 28 remaining states in which their SPM poverty rates were lower than their respective

---

[27] Significant differences based on a 90% statistical confidence level.

"official" poverty rates, nearly all (with Maine being the exception) were either in the South, or inland.

Figure 13. Difference in Poverty Rates by State Using the "Official"* Measure and the SPM: Three-Year Average 2010-2012

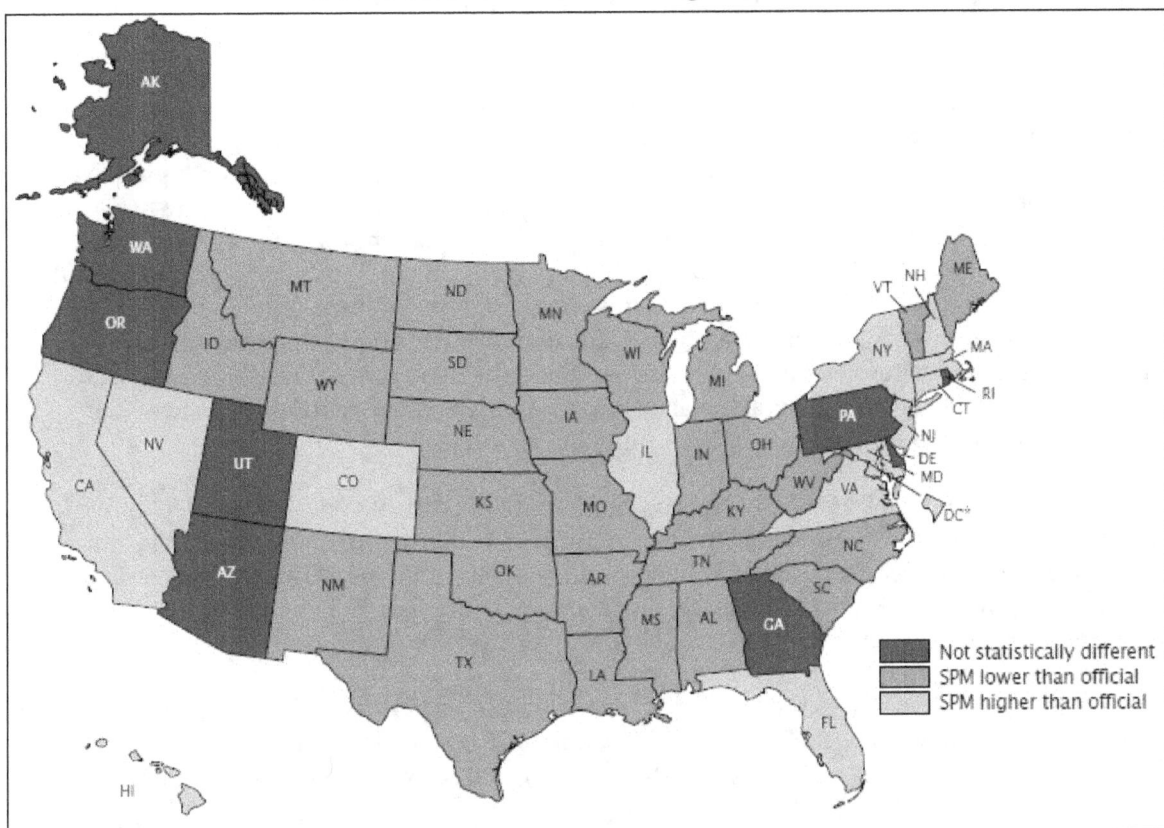

Source: Figure prepared by the Congressional Research Service (CRS), based on Kathleen Short, *The Research SUPPLEMENTAL POVERTY MEASURE: 2012*, U.S. Census Bureau, P60-247, Washington, DC, November 2013 http://www.census.gov/prod/2013pubs/p60-247.pdf.

Notes: Within state difference between official and SPM poverty rates determined at a 90% statistical confidence level.

* Differs from published "official" poverty rates as unrelated individuals under age 15 are included in the universe.

Figure 14 and **Figure 15** depict poverty rates by state under the official poverty measure and the SPM based on three years of CPS/ASEC data. Estimates are based on three-year (2010 to 2012) averages to improve the statistical reliability of estimates attainable from CPS/ASEC data at the state level. The two figures differ only in terms of the order in which states are sorted. In **Figure 14**, states are sorted from lowest to highest based on their respective "official" poverty rate point estimates, whereas in **Figure 15** states are sorted from lowest to highest based on their respective SPM poverty rate point estimates. In neither figure are precise rankings of states possible because of the depicted margin of error around each state's estimate. Within a state, a statistically significant difference[28] between a state's official poverty rate and its SPM poverty rate is signified

---

[28] Significant difference at a 90% statistical confidence level.

by solid-filled markers, indicating the point estimate under each measure, and a line connecting them, indicating the estimated difference (which is also shown in parentheses after each state name). The figures show the magnitude of the difference among the 13 states and the District of Columbia that had statistically significant higher poverty rates under the SPM than under the "official" measure, as well as for the 28 states in which the state's SPM rate was lower than its "official" poverty rate and the 9 states in which the incidence of poverty under the two measures did not differ statistically.

Differences in state poverty rates based on the SPM compared to the "official" measure may be due to a variety of factors. Geographic adjustments to SPM poverty income thresholds to account for differences in housing costs tend to result in higher poverty rates in areas with higher-priced housing than in areas with lower-priced housing. The mix of housing tenure (e.g., owner occupied, with or without a mortgage, renter occupied) may account for some of the difference between "official" and SPM poverty rates, within and between areas. Similarly, taxes may differ among areas. Also, populations may differ across areas in terms of household composition (e.g., share of households with cohabiting partners). The composition of the population based on age, or health insurance status, may also affect the incidence of SPM poverty relative to "official" poverty within and between geographic areas, by affecting medical out of pocket spending (MOOP), which is considered by SPM in estimating poverty.

Among the states with a statistically significant *increase* in poverty under the SPM, California's poverty rate increased by more than any other state's, increasing from 16.5% under the "official" measure to 23.8% under the SPM, or 7.3 percentage points. Under the "official" measure, California's poverty rate was substantially above the U.S. rate (15.1%), but under the SPM, California's poverty rate is estimated as the highest in the nation.

Other states with comparatively large increases in their poverty rates (in the four percentage point range) under the SPM compared to the "official" measure include Hawaii (an increase from 12.0% to 17.3%), Florida (a 15.5% to 19.5% increase), and New Jersey (a 10.7% to 15.5% increase).

Three states had decreases in their SPM poverty rate compared to their "official" rate in the four percentage point range. Mississippi and New Mexico, among the states with the highest "official" poverty (20.7% and 20.3%, respectively), both have an estimated SPM poverty rate of 16.1%— just about equal to the U.S. SPM rate (16.0%). West Virginia's "official" poverty rate (17.2%) is well above the "official" U.S. rate (15.1%), but its SPM rate (12.9%) falls well below the U.S. SPM rate (16.0%).

Figure 14. Poverty Rates by State Using the "Official"* Measure and the SPM: Three-Year Average 2010-2012

(States Ranked in Ascending Order by Official Poverty Rate; Percentage Point Difference in Parentheses)

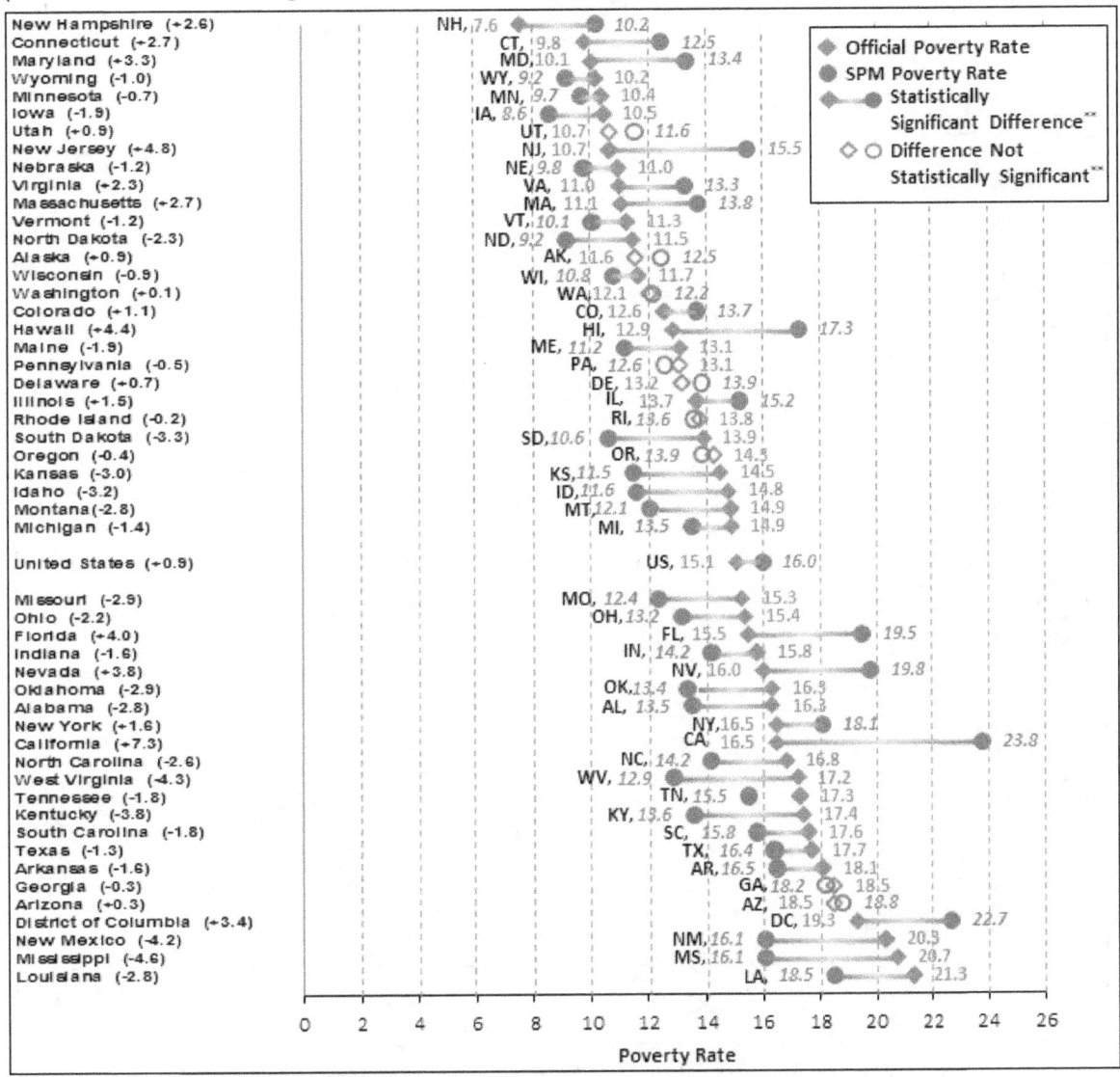

Source: Figure prepared by the Congressional Research Service (CRS), based on Kathleen Short, *The Research SUPPLEMENTAL POVERTY MEASURE: 2012*, U.S. Census Bureau, P60-247, Washington, DC, November 2013 http://www.census.gov/prod/2013pubs/p60-247.pdf.

* Differs from published "official" poverty rates as unrelated individuals under age 15 are included in the universe.

** Within state difference between official and SPM poverty rates determined at a 90% statistical confidence level.

Figure 15. Poverty Rates by State Using the "Official"* Measure and the SPM: Three-Year Average 2010-2012

(States Ranked in Ascending Order by SPM Poverty Rate; Percentage Point Difference in Parentheses)

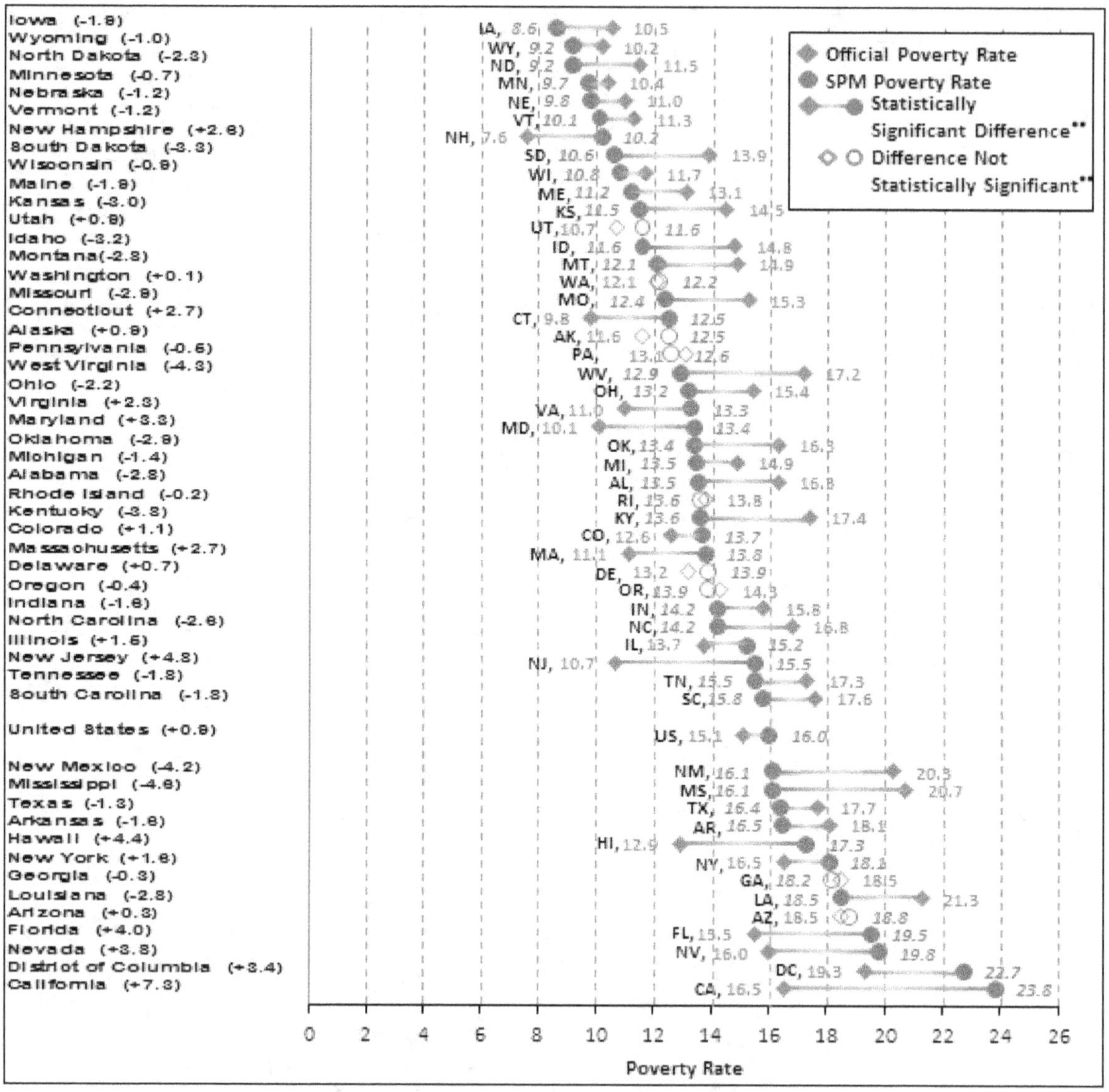

Source: Figure prepared by the Congressional Research Service (CRS), based on Kathleen Short, *The Research SUPPLEMENTAL POVERTY MEASURE: 2012*, U.S. Census Bureau, P60-247, Washington, DC, November 2013 http://www.census.gov/prod/2013pubs/p60-247.pdf

* Differs from published "official" poverty rates as unrelated individuals under age 15 are included in the universe.

** Within state difference between official and SPM poverty rates determined at a 90% statistical confidence level.

Marginal Effects of Counting Specified Resources and Expenses on Poverty Under the SPM

Figure 16 focuses strictly on the SPM, examining the marginal effects on poverty rates attributable to the inclusion of each selected income/resource or expenditure element on the measure. The marginal effects of each element on the SPM are displayed by age group. Elements that marginally contribute resources, and thereby have a poverty reducing effect when included in the SPM, are ranked from left to right in terms of their effect on poverty reduction among all persons. Similarly, expenditure elements, which are subtracted from resources and thereby marginally increase poverty as measured by the SPM, are ranked from left to right by their marginal poverty increasing effects on all persons.

The figure shows, for example, that the EITC has a greater poverty reducing effect than any of the other depicted resource elements. Overall, the EITC lowers the SPM poverty rate for all persons by 3.0 percentage points. The EITC is followed by SNAP benefits (1.6 percentage point reduction), housing subsidies (0.9 percentage point reduction), school lunch (0.4 percentage point reduction), and WIC and LIHEAP (each with a 0.1 percentage point reduction).

In contrast, on the expenditure side, child support paid to members outside the household has a relatively small effect on increasing the overall poverty rate. Federal income taxes before considering refundable credits, such as the EITC (counted on the resource side), result in an increase in overall poverty of 0.4 percentage points. FICA payroll taxes have a larger effect on marginal poverty (1.6 percentage point increase) than federal income taxes, as do work expenses (1.9 percentage points). Among all of the expense elements presented, medical out of pocket expenses (MOOP) contribute to the largest increase in poverty (3.4 percentage point increase for all persons).

Among the three age groups, the additional resources included in the SPM have a greater effect on reducing poverty among children (persons under age 18) and poverty among working age adults (ages 18 to 64) than on the aged (age 65 and older), with the exception of housing subsidies, which reduce the aged poverty rate by about the same amount as that of children. The EITC has a greater effect of reducing poverty among children (6.7 percentage point reduction) than any of the other added SPM resources.

On the expenditure side, FICA payroll taxes and work expenses have a greater effect on increasing poverty among children (due to a working parent) and non-aged adults than on the aged, who are less likely to be in the labor force and incur work-related taxes and expenses. Notably, under the SPM, MOOP expenses contribute to a substantial increase in poverty among the aged, contributing to a 6.4 percentage point increase in their poverty rate.

The relative distribution of additional resources and expenses in the SPM by age group helps to explain why poverty among children is lower under the SPM than it is under the "official" measure, whereas it is considerably higher for the aged.

Figure 16. Percentage Point Change in Poverty Rates Attributable to Selected Income and Expenditure Elements Under the Research Supplemental Poverty Measure, by Age Group: 2012

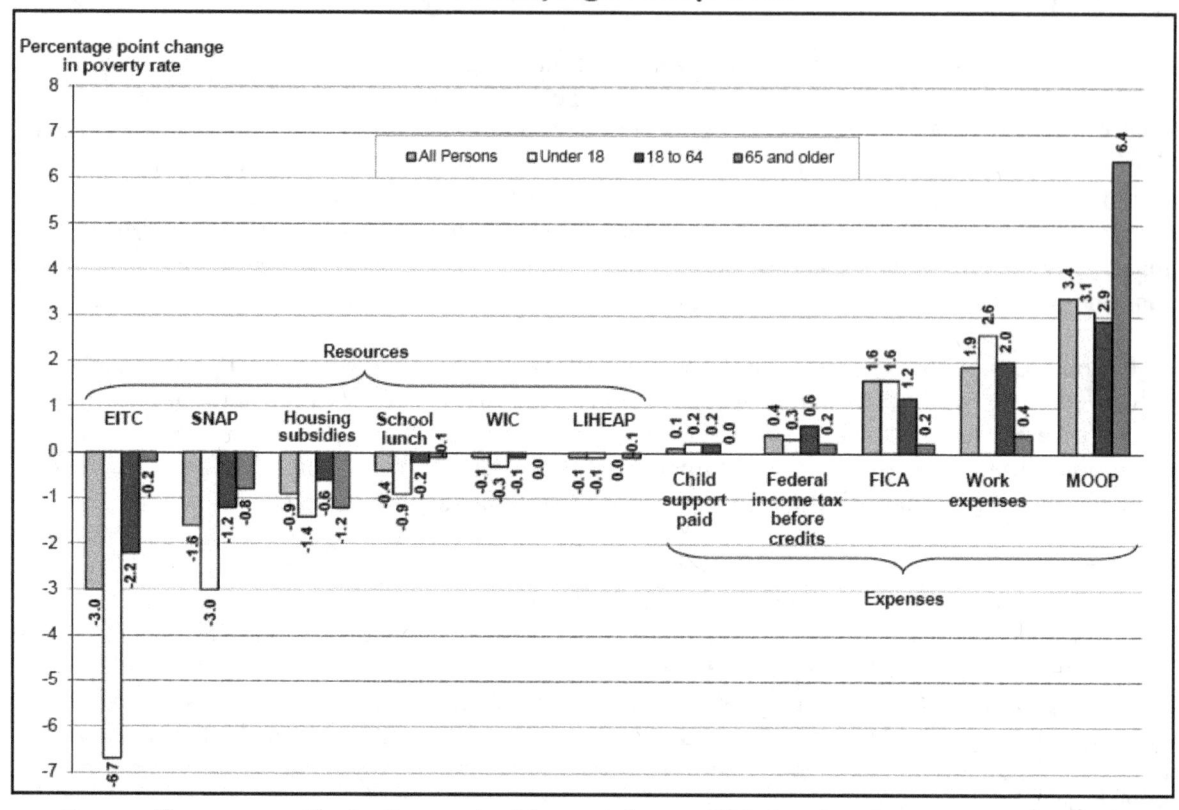

Source: Figure prepared by the Congressional Research Service (CRS), based on Kathleen Short, *The Research SUPPLEMENTAL POVERTY MEASURE: 2012*, U.S. Census Bureau, P60-247, Washington, DC, November 2013 http://www.census.gov/prod/2013pubs/p60-247.pdf.

Distribution of the Population by Ratio of Income/Resources Relative to Poverty

Figure 17 shows the distribution of the population by age group according to the degree to which their income and resources fall below or above poverty under the "official" and SPM definitions. The figure breaks out the poor population, depicted by brackets, into the share whose income and resources fall below half of their respective poverty lines (a classification sometimes referred to as "deep poverty") and the remainder. Others are categorized by the extent to which their income/resources exceed poverty under the two definitions, with those who fall below twice the poverty line also demarcated by brackets.

The figure shows, for example, that the share of children in "deep poverty" under the SPM is considerably lower than under the "official" measure (4.7% compared to 10.3%). As shown earlier, the SPM child poverty rate (18.0%) is lower than the "official" rate (22.3%). However, under the SPM, a much greater share of children live in "families" with income/resources between one and two times the poverty line than under the "official" measure (33.7% and 21.9%). Altogether, well over half of the children live in "families" having income/resources below twice the poverty line under the SPM (55.7%) compared to over two-fifths (44.2%) under the "official" measure. Thus, while the SPM appears to result in fewer children being counted as poor than under the "official" measure, under the SPM a greater share than under the "official" measure are concentrated at income levels just above poverty.

Among persons age 65 and over, a greater share are poor under the SPM than under the "official" measure, as shown earlier (14.8% compared to 9.1%), and a greater share are in "deep poverty" under the SPM (4.7%) than under the "official" measure (2.7%). In contrast to the "official" measure, under which about one-third (32.3%) of the aged have income below 200% of poverty, almost half (47.1%) have income/resources below that level under the SPM.

Figure 17. Distribution of the Population by Income/Resources to Poverty Ratios Under the "Official"* and Research Supplemental Poverty Measures, by Age Group: 2012

(Percent distribution)

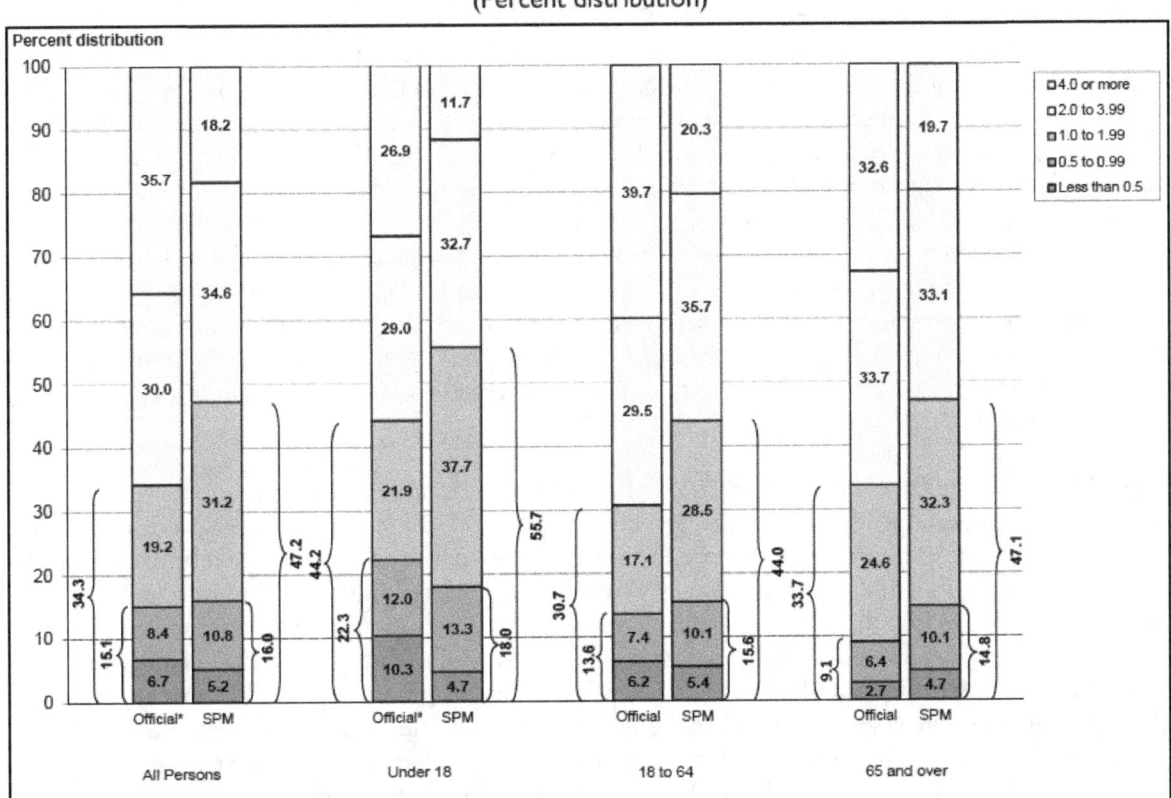

Source: Figure prepared by the Congressional Research Service (CRS), based on Kathleen Short, *The Research SUPPLEMENTAL POVERTY MEASURE: 2012*, U.S. Census Bureau, P60-247, Washington, DC, November 2013 http://www.census.gov/prod/2013pubs/p60-247.pdf.

* Differs from published "official" poverty rates as unrelated individuals under age 15 are included in the universe.

Discussion

As a research measure, the SPM offers potential for improved insight leading to better understanding of the nature and circumstances of those deemed to be among the nation's most economically and socially vulnerable. The SPM offers the means to better assess the performance of the economy, government policies, and programs with regard to the population's ability to secure sufficient income/resources to be able to meet basic expenditures for food, clothing, shelter, and utilities (plus "a little bit more").

The SPM counts considerably more elderly as poor than does the "official" measure. Medical expenses appear to be the driving factor in increasing poverty among the elderly under the SPM (see **Figure 16**). While not negating the improvement in the poverty status of the aged over the years, based on the "official" measure (see **Figure 2**), the SPM points more directly to the economic vulnerability of the aged, based not on income/resources alone, but rather, medical expenses competing for income that might otherwise be used to meet basic needs (i.e., FCSU plus "a little bit more"). Rising medical costs in society overall and individuals' personal health and insurance statuses pose potential economic risk to the aged being able to meet basic needs, as captured by FCSU-based poverty thresholds. The SPM provides additional insight that poverty reduction among the elderly depends not only on improving income, but also on their ability to reduce exposure to high medical expenses through "affordable" insurance. Rising medical costs in society also place the aged at increased risk of poverty under the SPM. It is worth noting that the SPM does not consider financial assets, other than interest, dividends, and annuity income from those assets, nor non-liquid assets (e.g., home equity) in determining poverty status. The SPM therefore does not address the means or extent to which the aged might tap those assets to meet medical or other needs.

The SPM results in fewer children being counted as poor than under the "official" measure. Still, the incidence of child poverty under the SPM, as under the "official" measure, exceeds that of the aged, but by a much slimmer margin (see **Figure 9**). Work-based supports, which both encourage work and help to offset the costs of going to work, appear be especially important to families with children, as captured by the SPM. The EITC, not counted under the "official" measure, significantly reduces child poverty as measured by the SPM, helping to offset taxes and work-related expenses working families with children incur (also captured by the SPM, but not under the "official" measure) (see **Figure 16**). The lack of safe, reliable, and affordable child care may limit parents' attachment to the labor force, contributing to poverty by reducing earnings that parents might otherwise secure. The SPM recognizes child care as a necessary expense many families face in their decisions relating to work by subtracting work-related child care expenses from income/resources that might otherwise go to meeting basic needs (i.e., FCSU plus "a little bit more"). As a consequence, the SPM should be sensitive to measuring the effects of child care programs and policies on child care affordability and poverty. The SPM captures the policy effects of assisting the poor through the provision of in-kind benefits, as opposed to just cash, whereas the "official" measure does not. For example, SNAP benefits, not captured under the "official" poverty measure, appear to have a sizeable effect in reducing child poverty under the SPM. Additionally, the expansion of the economic unit under the SPM to include cohabiting partners and their relatives may also contribute to lower child poverty rates under the SPM than under the "official" poverty measure, which is based on family ties defined by blood, marriage, and adoption.

Appendix A. U.S. Poverty Statistics: 1959-2013

Table A-1. Poverty Rates (Percent Poor) for Selected Groups, 1959-2013

| Year | All Persons | Related Children Under Age 18[a] | | | Adults | | Race/Ethnicity[b]—All Ages | | | | |
		Total	In Female-Headed Families	In All Other Families	Ages 18-64	Age 65+	White[b]	White Non-Hispanic[b]	Black[b]	Hispanic (any race)	Asian[b]
2013	14.5	19.5	45.8	10.7	13.6	9.5	12.3b	9.6b	27.2b	23.5b	10.5b
2012	15.0	21.3	47.2	12.5	13.7	9.1	12.7b	9.7b	27.2b	25.6	11.7b
2011	15.0	21.4	47.6	12.1	13.7	8.7	12.8b	9.8b	27.6b	25.3	12.3b
2010r	15.1	21.5	46.6	12.9	13.8	8.9	13.0b	9.9b	27.4b	26.5	12.2b
2009	14.3	20.1	44.4	12.3	12.9	8.9	12.3b	9.4b	25.8b	25.3	12.5b
2008	13.2	18.5	43.5	10.7	11.7	9.7	11.2b	8.6b	24.7b	23.2	11.8b
2007	12.5	17.6	43.0	9.5	10.9	9.7	10.5b	8.2b	24.5b	21.5	10.2b
2006	12.3	16.9	42.1	9.0	10.8	9.4	10.3b	8.2b	24.3b	20.6	10.3b
2005	12.6	17.1	42.8	9.3	11.1	10.1	10.6b	8.3b	24.9b	21.8	11.1b
2004r	12.7	17.3	41.9	9.7	11.3	9.8	10.8b	8.7b	24.7b	21.9	9.8b
2003	12.5	17.2	41.8	9.6	10.8	10.2	10.5b	8.2b	24.4b	22.5	11.8b
2002	12.1	16.3	39.6	9.2	10.6	10.4	10.2b	8.0b	24.1b	21.8	10.1b
2001	11.7	15.8	39.3	8.8	10.1	10.1	9.9	7.8	22.7	21.4	n/a
2000r	11.3	15.6	40.1	8.6	9.6	9.9	9.5	7.4	22.5	21.5	n/a
1999	11.8	16.3	41.9	9.0	10.0	9.7	9.8	7.7	23.6	22.8	n/a
1998	12.7	18.3	46.1	9.7	10.5	10.5	10.5	8.2	26.1	25.6	n/a
1997	13.3	19.2	49.0	10.2	10.9	10.5	11.0	8.6	26.5	27.1	n/a
1996	13.7	19.8	49.3	10.9	11.3	10.8	11.2	8.6	28.4	29.4	n/a
1995	13.8	20.2	50.3	10.7	11.4	10.5	11.2	8.5	29.3	30.3	n/a
1994	14.5	21.2	52.9	11.7	11.9	11.7	11.7	9.4	30.6	30.7	n/a
1993	15.1	22.0	53.7	12.4	12.4	12.2	12.2	9.9	33.1	30.6	n/a
1992r	14.8	21.6	54.6	11.8	11.9	12.9	11.9	9.6	33.4	29.6	n/a
1991r	14.2	21.1	55.5	11.1	11.4	12.4	11.3	9.4	32.7	28.7	n/a
1990	13.5	19.9	53.4	10.7	10.7	12.2	10.7	8.8	31.9	28.1	n/a
1989	12.8	19.0	51.1	10.4	10.2	11.4	10.0	8.3	30.7	26.2	n/a
1988r	13.0	19.0	52.9	10.0	10.5	12.0	10.1	8.4	31.3	26.7	n/a
1987r	13.4	19.7	54.7	10.9	10.6	12.5	10.4	8.7	32.4	28.0	n/a
1986	13.6	19.8	54.4	10.8	10.8	12.4	11.0	9.4	31.1	27.3	n/a
1985	14.0	20.1	53.6	11.7	11.3	12.6	11.4	9.7	31.3	29.0	n/a
1984	14.4	21.0	54.0	12.5	11.7	12.4	11.5	10.0	33.8	28.4	n/a

Year	All Persons	Related Children Under Age 18[a]			Adults		Race/Ethnicity[b]—All Ages				
		Total	In Female-Headed Families	In All Other Families	Ages 18-64	Age 65+	White[b]	White Non-Hispanic[b]	Black[b]	Hispanic (any race)	Asian[b]
1983	15.2	21.8	55.5	13.5	12.4	13.8	12.2	10.8	35.7	28.1	n/a
1982	15.0	21.3	56.0	13.0	12.0	14.6	12.0	10.6	35.6	29.9	n/a
1981	14.0	19.5	52.3	11.6	11.1	15.3	11.1	9.9	34.2	26.5	n/a
1980	13.0	17.9	50.8	10.4	10.1	15.7	10.2	9.1	32.5	25.7	n/a
1979	11.7	16.0	48.6	8.5	8.9	15.2	9.0	8.1	31.0	21.8	n/a
1978	11.4	15.7	50.6	7.9	8.7	14.0	8.7	7.9	30.6	21.6	n/a
1977	11.6	16.0	50.3	8.5	8.8	14.1	8.9	8.0	31.3	22.4	n/a
1976	11.8	15.8	52.0	8.5	9.0	15.0	9.1	8.1	31.1	24.7	n/a
1975	12.3	16.8	52.7	9.8	9.2	15.3	9.7	8.6	31.3	26.9	n/a
1974	11.2	15.1	51.5	8.3	8.3	14.6	8.6	7.7	30.3	23.0	n/a
1973	11.1	14.2	52.1	7.6	8.3	16.3	8.4	7.5	31.4	21.9	n/a
1972	11.9	14.9	53.1	8.6	8.8	18.6	9.0	n/a	33.3	n/a	n/a
1971	12.5	15.1	53.1	9.3	9.3	21.6	9.9	n/a	32.5	n/a	n/a
1970	12.6	14.9	53.0	9.2	9.0	24.6	9.9	n/a	33.5	n/a	n/a
1969	12.1	13.8	54.4	8.6	8.7	25.3	9.5	n/a	32.2	n/a	n/a
1968	12.8	15.3	55.2	10.2	9.0	25.0	10.0	n/a	34.7	n/a	n/a
1967	14.2	16.3	54.3	11.5	10.0	29.5	11.0	n/a	39.3	n/a	n/a
1966	14.7	17.4	58.2	12.6	10.5	28.5	11.3	n/a	41.8	n/a	n/a
1959	22.4	26.9	72.2	22.4	17.0	35.2	18.1	n/a	55.1	n/a	n/a

Source: Prepared by the Congressional Research Service using U.S. Bureau of the Census data based on the "official" measure of poverty.

Notes: r = revised estimates. n/a = not available.

a. Beginning in 1979, restricted to children in primary families only. Before 1979, includes children in unrelated subfamilies.

b. Beginning in 2002, CPS respondents could identify themselves as being of more than one race. Consequently, racial data for 2002 and after are not comparable to earlier years. Here, in 2002 and after, the term white means of white race alone, the term black means of black race alone, and the term Asian means Asian alone. Hispanics, who may be of any race, are included among whites and blacks unless otherwise noted.

Appendix B. Metropolitan Area Poverty Estimates

Table B-1. Metropolitan Area Poverty: 2013

Metropolitan Area	Total Population	Number Poor		Poverty Rate (Percent Poor)		
		Estimate	Margin of Error[a]	Poverty Rate	Margin of Error[a]	Rank[b]
Abilene, TX	154,458	26,016	+/-3,491	16.8%	+/-2.2%	169
Akron, OH	690,331	106,377	+/-7,877	15.4%	+/-1.1%	237
Albany, GA	150,485	37,441	+/-4,405	24.9%	+/-2.8%	15
Albany, OR	117,252	23,986	+/-4,096	20.5%	+/-3.5%	60
Albany-Schenectady-Troy, NY	846,922	105,640	+/-8,545	12.5%	+/-1.0%	320
Albuquerque, NM	890,054	173,028	+/-10,925	19.4%	+/-1.2%	86
Alexandria, LA	147,861	27,656	+/-3,989	18.7%	+/-2.7%	110
Allentown-Bethlehem-Easton, PA-NJ	804,393	99,692	+/-6,980	12.4%	+/-0.9%	324
Altoona, PA	123,730	20,392	+/-3,212	16.5%	+/-2.6%	182
Amarillo, TX	249,194	39,748	+/-3,969	16.0%	+/-1.6%	212
Ames, IA	84,045	19,770	+/-2,273	23.5%	+/-2.6%	22
Anchorage, AK	386,833	27,596	+/-3,586	7.1%	+/-0.9%	379
Ann Arbor, MI	335,915	56,191	+/-5,089	16.7%	+/-1.5%	175
Anniston-Oxford-Jacksonville, AL	113,722	24,825	+/-3,340	21.8%	+/-2.9%	38
Appleton, WI	226,221	18,291	+/-2,940	8.1%	+/-1.3%	376
Asheville, NC	429,282	68,399	+/-5,793	15.9%	+/-1.4%	214
Athens-Clarke County, GA	186,981	53,388	+/-5,015	28.6%	+/-2.6%	6
Atlanta-Sandy Springs-Roswell, GA	5,430,037	865,858	+/-28,129	15.9%	+/-0.5%	213
Atlantic City-Hammonton, NJ	270,136	48,716	+/-5,187	18.0%	+/-1.9%	123
Auburn-Opelika, AL	144,867	30,038	+/-4,160	20.7%	+/-2.9%	56
Augusta-Richmond County, GA-SC	565,819	111,863	+/-8,976	19.8%	+/-1.6%	80
Austin-Round Rock, TX	1,841,572	262,644	+/-14,918	14.3%	+/-0.8%	281
Bakersfield, CA	831,344	189,484	+/-13,393	22.8%	+/-1.6%	26
Baltimore-Columbia-Towson, MD	2,702,706	301,630	+/-13,812	11.2%	+/-0.5%	344
Bangor, ME	146,466	23,644	+/-3,195	16.1%	+/-2.2%	200
Barnstable Town, MA	212,139	19,313	+/-2,984	9.1%	+/-1.4%	368

CRS-47

Metropolitan Area	Total Population	Number Poor		Poverty Rate (Percent Poor)		
		Estimate	Margin of Error[a]	Poverty Rate	Margin of Error[a]	Rank[b]
Baton Rouge, LA	797,912	149,025	+/-10,622	18.7%	+/-1.3%	111
Battle Creek, MI	130,542	24,261	+/-3,240	18.6%	+/-2.4%	113
Bay City, MI	105,498	18,310	+/-2,533	17.4%	+/-2.4%	145
Beaumont-Port Arthur, TX	387,482	72,048	+/-7,227	18.6%	+/-1.8%	112
Beckley, WV	118,651	25,833	+/-3,422	21.8%	+/-2.8%	40
Bellingham, WA	200,426	34,135	+/-4,708	17.0%	+/-2.3%	160
Bend-Redmond, OR	164,655	26,397	+/-4,828	16.0%	+/-2.9%	207
Billings, MT	161,276	20,745	+/-2,832	12.9%	+/-1.7%	310
Binghamton, NY	236,898	38,784	+/-4,249	16.4%	+/-1.8%	189
Birmingham-Hoover, AL	1,116,257	188,610	+/-9,521	16.9%	+/-0.9%	166
Bismarck, ND	121,277	10,119	+/-1,758	8.3%	+/-1.5%	374
Blacksburg-Christiansburg-Radford, VA	166,843	37,896	+/-4,544	22.7%	+/-2.6%	27
Bloomington, IL	184,309	27,681	+/-3,555	15.0%	+/-1.9%	249
Bloomington, IN	148,709	33,760	+/-3,426	22.7%	+/-2.2%	28
Bloomsburg-Berwick, PA	80,653	13,275	+/-2,443	16.5%	+/-3.0%	183
Boise City, ID	637,683	107,713	+/-12,906	16.9%	+/-2.0%	167
Boston-Cambridge-Newton, MA-NH	4,525,102	470,178	+/-18,981	10.4%	+/-0.4%	357
Boulder, CO	300,101	41,700	+/-4,077	13.9%	+/-1.4%	287
Bowling Green, KY	156,092	30,727	+/-3,873	19.7%	+/-2.4%	82
Bremerton-Silverdale, WA	245,971	27,727	+/-4,028	11.3%	+/-1.6%	342
Bridgeport-Stamford-Norwalk, CT	921,302	88,808	+/-6,895	9.6%	+/-0.7%	359
Brownsville-Harlingen, TX	412,432	134,170	+/-8,943	32.5%	+/-2.2%	2
Brunswick, GA	111,440	22,111	+/-4,204	19.8%	+/-3.8%	76
Buffalo-Cheektowaga-Niagara Falls, NY	1,103,165	164,100	+/-8,568	14.9%	+/-0.8%	257
Burlington, NC	150,206	31,103	+/-4,266	20.7%	+/-2.8%	57
Burlington-South Burlington, VT	205,647	21,596	+/-3,045	10.5%	+/-1.5%	353
California-Lexington Park, MD	106,530	6,831	+/-2,204	6.4%	+/-2.1%	381
Canton-Massillon, OH	394,097	61,713	+/-5,716	15.7%	+/-1.4%	223
Cape Coral-Fort Myers, FL	649,199	107,225	+/-8,880	16.5%	+/-1.4%	181
Cape Girardeau, MO-IL	91,588	16,457	+/-2,819	18.0%	+/-2.9%	124
Carbondale-Marion, IL	120,496	27,530	+/-3,465	22.8%	+/-2.8%	25

Metropolitan Area	Total Population	Number Poor		Poverty Rate (Percent Poor)		
		Estimate	Margin of Error[a]	Poverty Rate	Margin of Error[a]	Rank[b]
Carson City, NV	52,168	7,885	+/-2,319	15.1%	+/-4.4%	245
Casper, WY	79,240	7,448	+/-1,658	9.4%	+/-2.1%	364
Cedar Rapids, IA	255,759	23,609	+/-3,504	9.2%	+/-1.4%	367
Chambersburg-Waynesboro, PA	148,856	19,211	+/-3,790	12.9%	+/-2.5%	305
Champaign-Urbana, IL	217,009	44,185	+/-3,690	20.4%	+/-1.7%	62
Charleston, WV	220,824	36,049	+/-4,747	16.3%	+/-2.1%	191
Charleston-North Charleston, SC	693,815	112,715	+/-7,581	16.2%	+/-1.1%	194
Charlotte-Concord-Gastonia, NC-SC	2,298,466	339,434	+/-15,265	14.8%	+/-0.7%	263
Charlottesville, VA	211,108	33,811	+/-4,219	16.0%	+/-2.0%	208
Chattanooga, TN-GA	527,350	85,002	+/-7,650	16.1%	+/-1.4%	202
Cheyenne, WY	93,972	8,952	+/-2,894	9.5%	+/-3.1%	361
Chicago-Naperville-Elgin, IL-IN-WI	9,375,444	1,347,179	+/-32,543	14.4%	+/-0.3%	277
Chico, CA	217,808	46,895	+/-5,012	21.5%	+/-2.3%	45
Cincinnati, OH-KY-IN	2,084,132	301,214	+/-13,602	14.5%	+/-0.7%	273
Clarksville, TN-KY	262,145	42,952	+/-4,799	16.4%	+/-1.8%	187
Cleveland, TN	116,431	23,016	+/-4,071	19.8%	+/-3.5%	81
Cleveland-Elyria, OH	2,023,498	315,381	+/-14,229	15.6%	+/-0.7%	226
Coeur d'Alene, ID	142,546	17,161	+/-3,928	12.0%	+/-2.8%	330
College Station-Bryan, TX	224,477	63,800	+/-6,284	28.4%	+/-2.8%	7
Colorado Springs, CO	660,782	71,297	+/-7,162	10.8%	+/-1.1%	350
Columbia, MO	161,119	34,118	+/-3,949	21.2%	+/-2.4%	52
Columbia, SC	757,614	125,517	+/-9,093	16.6%	+/-1.2%	180
Columbus, GA-AL	299,327	64,754	+/-6,177	21.6%	+/-2.0%	43
Columbus, IN	77,877	9,387	+/-2,413	12.1%	+/-3.1%	329
Columbus, OH	1,913,546	283,702	+/-15,369	14.8%	+/-0.8%	258
Corpus Christi, TX	436,129	75,592	+/-7,264	17.3%	+/-1.6%	146
Corvallis, OR	81,212	18,762	+/-2,296	23.1%	+/-2.8%	23
Crestview-Fort Walton Beach-Destin, FL	246,364	38,598	+/-5,626	15.7%	+/-2.3%	222
Cumberland, MD-WV	93,006	16,404	+/-2,954	17.6%	+/-3.2%	136
Dallas-Fort Worth-Arlington, TX	6,724,464	1,005,325	+/-30,615	15.0%	+/-0.5%	253
Dalton, GA	140,291	30,592	+/-4,719	21.8%	+/-3.4%	39

Metropolitan Area	Total Population	Number Poor		Poverty Rate (Percent Poor)		
		Estimate	Margin of Error[a]	Poverty Rate	Margin of Error[a]	Rank[b]
Danville, IL	77,461	14,964	+/-2,398	19.3%	+/-3.1%	90
Daphne-Fairhope-Foley, AL	192,943	28,028	+/-5,351	14.5%	+/-2.8%	270
Davenport-Mo ine-Rock Island, IA-IL	373,851	54,024	+/-5,283	14.5%	+/-1.4%	274
Dayton, OH	776,921	127,254	+/-9,611	16.4%	+/-1.2%	188
Decatur, AL	150,726	26,408	+/-3,888	17.5%	+/-2.6%	139
Decatur, IL	105,437	19,243	+/-3,025	18.3%	+/-2.9%	119
Deltona-Daytona Beach-Ormond Beach, FL	589,119	95,566	+/-8,042	16.2%	+/-1.4%	195
Denver-Aurora-Lakewood, CO	2,663,509	323,179	+/-15,703	12.1%	+/-0.6%	328
Des Moines-West Des Moines, IA	588,147	64,790	+/-5,793	11.0%	+/-1.0%	346
Detroit-Warren-Dearborn, MI	4,252,247	717,584	+/-17,780	16.9%	+/-0.4%	168
Dothan, AL	146,190	26,816	+/-2,595	18.3%	+/-1.8%	116
Dover, DE	164,302	20,334	+/-3,558	12.4%	+/-2.2%	325
Dubuque, IA	92,158	12,633	+/-1,868	13.7%	+/-2.0%	291
Duluth, MN-WI	269,518	45,693	+/-4,614	17.0%	+/-1.7%	163
Durham-Chapel Hill, NC	510,288	86,378	+/-6,899	16.9%	+/-1.3%	165
East Stroudsburg, PA	164,528	17,845	+/-3,781	10.8%	+/-2.3%	349
Eau Claire, WI	157,876	18,956	+/-3,155	12.0%	+/-2.0%	332
El Centro, CA	165,902	36,645	+/-5,905	22.1%	+/-3.5%	35
El Paso, TX	816,158	184,427	+/-12,589	22.6%	+/-1.5%	30
E izabethtown-Fort Knox, KY	147,225	23,253	+/-3,377	15.8%	+/-2.3%	220
E khart-Goshen, IN	195,903	31,743	+/-5,292	16.2%	+/-2.7%	197
Elmira, NY	83,345	14,217	+/-2,131	17.1%	+/-2.6%	158
Erie, PA	267,946	49,005	+/-5,936	18.3%	+/-2.2%	118
Eugene, OR	349,317	75,232	+/-7,088	21.5%	+/-2.0%	44
Evansville, IN-KY	305,403	49,315	+/-5,336	16.1%	+/-1.7%	199
Fairbanks, AK	96,578	7,442	+/-2,543	7.7%	+/-2.6%	378
Fargo, ND-MN	214,216	29,879	+/-3,940	13.9%	+/-1.8%	285
Farmington, NM	125,488	28,442	+/-4,450	22.7%	+/-3.5%	29
Fayetteville, NC	365,455	68,554	+/-5,288	18.8%	+/-1.4%	106
Fayetteville-Springdale-Rogers, AR-MO	480,149	80,859	+/-8,372	16.8%	+/-1.7%	170
Flagstaff, AZ	127,378	30,726	+/-3,789	24.1%	+/-2.9%	17

Metropolitan Area	Total Population	Number Poor		Poverty Rate (Percent Poor)		
		Estimate	Margin of Error[a]	Poverty Rate	Margin of Error[a]	Rank[b]
Flint, MI	409,193	88,579	+/-7,484	21.6%	+/-1.8%	42
Florence, SC	201,368	46,093	+/-5,753	22.9%	+/-2.9%	24
Florence-Muscle Shoals, AL	144,987	23,034	+/-2,993	15.9%	+/-2.1%	218
Fond du Lac, WI	98,663	8,023	+/-1,707	8.1%	+/-1.7%	375
Fort Colins, CO	307,412	43,846	+/-4,203	14.3%	+/-1.4%	280
Fort Smith, AR-OK	275,581	65,557	+/-6,172	23.8%	+/-2.2%	19
Fort Wayne, IN	416,163	66,755	+/-5,712	16.0%	+/-1.4%	206
Fresno, CA	937,990	270,072	+/-12,767	28.8%	+/-1.4%	5
Gadsden, AL	102,633	19,363	+/-3,161	18.9%	+/-3.1%	102
Gainesville, FL	256,894	68,758	+/-5,496	26.8%	+/-2.1%	10
Gainesville, GA	185,118	40,630	+/-5,458	21.9%	+/-2.9%	37
Gettysburg, PA	97,009	8,620	+/-2,132	8.9%	+/-2.2%	372
Glens Falls, NY	124,199	15,784	+/-2,676	12.7%	+/-2.2%	316
Goldsboro, NC	120,867	25,910	+/-5,137	21.4%	+/-4.2%	47
Grand Forks, ND-MN	94,728	14,555	+/-1,687	15.4%	+/-1.8%	238
Grand Island, NE	81,981	12,340	+/-2,849	15.1%	+/-3.5%	246
Grand Junction, CO	143,253	23,910	+/-4,425	16.7%	+/-3.1%	176
Grand Rapids-Wyoming, MI	993,281	139,139	+/-8,997	14.0%	+/-0.9%	284
Grants Pass, OR	82,361	14,035	+/-3,095	17.0%	+/-3.8%	159
Great Falls, MT	80,102	12,814	+/-2,715	16.0%	+/-3.4%	210
Greeley, CO	263,036	35,126	+/-4,926	13.4%	+/-1.9%	300
Green Bay, WI	304,580	36,549	+/-5,101	12.0%	+/-1.7%	333
Greensboro-High Point, NC	722,405	143,646	+/-9,658	19.9%	+/-1.3%	75
Greenville, NC	168,611	43,223	+/-5,197	25.6%	+/-3.1%	11
Greenville-Anderson-Mauldin, SC	826,492	143,919	+/-11,385	17.4%	+/-1.4%	142
Gulfport-Biloxi-Pascagoula, MS	375,050	72,312	+/-7,842	19.3%	+/-2.1%	93
Hagerstown-Martinsburg, MD-WV	246,865	30,667	+/-4,873	12.4%	+/-2.0%	322
Hammond, LA	121,122	26,234	+/-4,042	21.7%	+/-3.3%	41
Hanford-Corcoran, CA	133,031	28,473	+/-5,298	21.4%	+/-4.0%	48
Harrisburg-Carlisle, PA	538,015	61,268	+/-5,964	11.4%	+/-1.1%	339
Harrisonburg, VA	119,953	20,308	+/-3,245	16.9%	+/-2.7%	164

| | | Number Poor | | Poverty Rate (Percent Poor) | | |
Metropolitan Area	Total Population	Estimate	Margin of Error[a]	Poverty Rate	Margin of Error[a]	Rank[b]
Hartford-West Hartford-East Hartford, CT	1,169,485	125,923	+/-9,009	10.8%	+/-0.8%	351
Hattiesburg, MS	144,861	34,291	+/-4,546	23.7%	+/-3.1%	20
Hickory-Lenoir-Morganton, NC	356,214	61,715	+/-6,542	17.3%	+/-1.8%	148
Hilton Head Island-Bluffton-Beaufort, SC	192,499	30,949	+/-5,259	16.1%	+/-2.7%	204
Hinesville, GA	79,128	16,111	+/-3,079	20.4%	+/-3.9%	63
Homosassa Springs, FL	136,633	22,952	+/-3,284	16.8%	+/-2.4%	172
Hot Springs, AR	94,437	22,668	+/-3,723	24.0%	+/-3.9%	18
Houma-Thibodaux, LA	205,658	27,916	+/-4,139	13.6%	+/-2.0%	292
Houston-The Woodlands-Sugar Land, TX	6,228,091	1,021,922	+/-32,157	16.4%	+/-0.5%	184
Huntington-Ashland, WV-KY-OH	354,931	71,701	+/-6,538	20.2%	+/-1.8%	67
Huntsville, AL	423,978	63,797	+/-6,818	15.0%	+/-1.6%	247
Idaho Falls, ID	135,972	15,189	+/-3,087	11.2%	+/-2.3%	343
Indianapolis-Carmel-Anderson, IN	1,909,800	290,647	+/-12,942	15.2%	+/-0.7%	242
Iowa City, IA	152,657	23,856	+/-3,159	15.6%	+/-2.1%	224
Ithaca, NY	88,377	17,907	+/-2,704	20.3%	+/-2.9%	66
Jackson, MI	150,916	29,064	+/-3,814	19.3%	+/-2.5%	94
Jackson, MS	557,607	122,754	+/-7,806	22.0%	+/-1.4%	36
Jackson, TN	125,360	26,178	+/-3,335	20.9%	+/-2.7%	54
Jacksonville, FL	1,366,441	202,025	+/-12,483	14.8%	+/-0.9%	262
Jacksonville, NC	170,510	28,935	+/-4,900	17.0%	+/-2.8%	161
Janesville-Beloit, WI	156,924	22,915	+/-4,090	14.6%	+/-2.6%	268
Jefferson City, MO	138,359	18,375	+/-3,729	13.3%	+/-2.7%	302
Johnson City, TN	193,692	37,292	+/-4,251	19.3%	+/-2.1%	95
Johnstown, PA	132,298	21,707	+/-2,741	16.4%	+/-2.1%	185
Jonesboro, AR	121,308	25,933	+/-3,668	21.4%	+/-3.1%	50
Joplin, MO	171,028	29,190	+/-4,347	17.1%	+/-2.6%	157
Kahului-Wailuku-Lahaina, HI	158,710	15,013	+/-2,564	9.5%	+/-1.6%	362
Kalamazoo-Portage, MI	322,236	57,240	+/-5,097	17.8%	+/-1.6%	129
Kankakee, IL	107,450	18,358	+/-3,669	17.1%	+/-3.4%	155
Kansas City, MO-KS	2,018,783	255,291	+/-12,778	12.6%	+/-0.6%	318
Kennewick-Richland, WA	266,874	38,878	+/-5,751	14.6%	+/-2.2%	269

Metropolitan Area	Total Population	Number Poor		Poverty Rate (Percent Poor)		
		Estimate	Margin of Error[a]	Poverty Rate	Margin of Error[a]	Rank[b]
Killeen-Temple, TX	401,026	57,065	+/-7,797	14.2%	+/-1.9%	282
Kingsport-Bristol-Bristol, TN-VA	302,495	54,895	+/-5,958	18.1%	+/-2.0%	121
Kingston, NY	173,358	19,549	+/-4,087	11.3%	+/-2.4%	341
Knoxville, TN	831,129	145,567	+/-9,055	17.5%	+/-1.1%	140
Kokomo, IN	81,130	12,612	+/-2,234	15.5%	+/-2.7%	228
La Crosse-Onalaska, WI-MN	130,300	20,554	+/-3,101	15.8%	+/-2.4%	221
Lafayette, LA	468,912	76,884	+/-8,310	16.4%	+/-1.8%	186
Lafayette-West Lafayette, IN	194,061	37,427	+/-5,210	19.3%	+/-2.6%	92
Lake Charles, LA	198,778	30,927	+/-4,825	15.6%	+/-2.4%	227
Lake Havasu City-Kingman, AZ	195,730	41,429	+/-6,226	21.2%	+/-3.1%	53
Lakeland-Winter Haven, FL	608,424	118,007	+/-11,131	19.4%	+/-1.8%	87
Lancaster, PA	514,196	53,694	+/-5,804	10.4%	+/-1.1%	355
Lansing-East Lansing, MI	447,127	80,872	+/-7,023	18.1%	+/-1.6%	122
Laredo, TX	258,684	80,403	+/-7,285	31.1%	+/-2.8%	3
Las Cruces, NM	208,101	57,908	+/-6,390	27.8%	+/-3.1%	8
Las Vegas-Henderson-Paradise, NV	2,002,803	321,455	+/-16,823	16.1%	+/-0.8%	205
Lawrence, KS	105,235	17,967	+/-4,054	17.1%	+/-3.8%	156
Lawton, OK	121,949	24,842	+/-3,444	20.4%	+/-2.8%	61
Lebanon, PA	131,958	14,367	+/-2,930	10.9%	+/-2.2%	348
Lewiston, ID-WA	60,924	8,151	+/-2,133	13.4%	+/-3.5%	299
Lewiston-Auburn, ME	104,601	17,884	+/-3,007	17.1%	+/-2.9%	154
Lexington-Fayette, KY	472,058	80,728	+/-6,536	17.1%	+/-1.4%	153
Lima, OH	101,118	15,154	+/-2,407	15.0%	+/-2.4%	251
Lincoln, NE	302,836	46,833	+/-5,684	15.5%	+/-1.8%	232
Little Rock-North Little Rock-Conway, AR	711,357	107,972	+/-9,231	15.2%	+/-1.3%	244
Logan, UT-ID	125,695	18,371	+/-3,207	14.6%	+/-2.5%	266
Longview, TX	207,330	39,098	+/-5,262	18.9%	+/-2.5%	103
Longview, WA	100,113	14,491	+/-3,004	14.5%	+/-3.0%	272
Los Angeles-Long Beach-Anaheim, CA	12,940,754	2,283,272	+/-40,149	17.6%	+/-0.3%	135
Louisville/Jefferson County, KY-IN	1,237,895	171,328	+/-12,460	13.8%	+/-1.0%	288
Lubbock, TX	292,742	51,653	+/-5,743	17.6%	+/-1.9%	134

Metropolitan Area	Total Population	Number Poor		Poverty Rate (Percent Poor)		
		Estimate	Margin of Error[a]	Poverty Rate	Margin of Error[a]	Rank[b]
Lynchburg, VA	247,740	38,287	+/-5,316	15.5%	+/-2.1%	234
Macon, GA	221,779	55,647	+/-5,641	25.1%	+/-2.5%	14
Madera, CA	144,954	34,242	+/-5,853	23.6%	+/-4.0%	21
Madison, WI	612,386	82,323	+/-6,973	13.4%	+/-1.1%	297
Manchester-Nashua, NH	395,786	38,127	+/-5,228	9.6%	+/-1.3%	360
Manhattan, KS	88,998	18,070	+/-2,763	20.3%	+/-3.0%	65
Mankato-North Mankato, MN	92,795	15,470	+/-2,101	16.7%	+/-2.2%	177
Mansfield, OH	114,496	20,114	+/-3,059	17.6%	+/-2.6%	138
McAllen-Edinburg-Mission, TX	803,934	275,681	+/-16,441	34.3%	+/-2.0%	1
Medford, OR	205,687	38,784	+/-7,040	18.9%	+/-3.4%	104
Memphis, TN-MS-AR	1,319,206	261,291	+/-11,676	19.8%	+/-0.9%	77
Merced, CA	256,177	64,552	+/-6,551	25.2%	+/-2.6%	13
Miami-Fort Lauderdale-West Palm Beach, FL	5,751,004	1,017,832	+/-27,848	17.7%	+/-0.5%	131
Michigan City-La Porte, IN	101,722	17,699	+/-3,213	17.4%	+/-3.2%	143
Midland, MI	82,183	13,625	+/-2,449	16.6%	+/-3.0%	179
Midland, TX	153,451	14,293	+/-3,501	9.3%	+/-2.3%	366
Milwaukee-Waukesha-West Allis, WI	1,539,233	244,752	+/-10,718	15.9%	+/-0.7%	217
Minneapolis-St. Paul-Bloomington, MN-WI	3,397,278	349,161	+/-13,880	10.3%	+/-0.4%	358
Missoula, MT	108,797	19,469	+/-3,626	17.9%	+/-3.3%	125
Mobile, AL	404,637	80,960	+/-7,633	20.0%	+/-1.9%	72
Modesto, CA	518,152	114,628	+/-9,386	22.1%	+/-1.8%	34
Monroe, LA	168,802	42,735	+/-5,063	25.3%	+/-3.0%	12
Monroe, MI	147,322	18,984	+/-2,984	12.9%	+/-2.0%	307
Montgomery, AL	363,458	69,589	+/-6,497	19.1%	+/-1.8%	97
Morgantown, WV	126,795	24,361	+/-2,922	19.2%	+/-2.3%	96
Morristown, TN	112,273	19,831	+/-3,735	17.7%	+/-3.3%	133
Mount Vernon-Anacortes, WA	116,391	20,682	+/-3,644	17.8%	+/-3.1%	128
Muncie, IN	110,512	24,950	+/-2,907	22.6%	+/-2.6%	31
Muskegon, MI	163,873	33,809	+/-3,737	20.6%	+/-2.3%	59
Myrtle Beach-Conway-North Myrtle Beach, SC-NC	400,485	73,380	+/-6,568	18.3%	+/-1.6%	117
Napa, CA	136,394	12,286	+/-2,875	9.0%	+/-2.1%	369

Metropolitan Area	Total Population	Number Poor		Poverty Rate (Percent Poor)		
		Estimate	Margin of Error[a]	Poverty Rate	Margin of Error[a]	Rank[b]
Naples-Immokalee-Marco Island, FL	336,570	43,152	+/-6,178	12.8%	+/-1.8%	311
Nashville-Davidson—Murfreesboro—Franklin, TN	1,718,322	235,823	+/-13,134	13.7%	+/-0.8%	290
New Bern, NC	124,576	19,936	+/-3,616	16.0%	+/-2.8%	209
New Haven-Mi ford, CT	836,150	107,710	+/-8,771	12.9%	+/-1.0%	308
New Orleans-Metairie, LA	1,221,794	235,888	+/-11,662	19.3%	+/-1.0%	91
New York-Newark-Jersey City, NY-NJ-PA	19,589,817	2,861,640	+/-41,911	14.6%	+/-0.2%	267
Niles-Benton Harbor, MI	150,975	24,561	+/-2,696	16.3%	+/-1.8%	193
North Port-Sarasota-Bradenton, FL	722,807	103,748	+/-8,231	14.4%	+/-1.1%	278
Norwich-New London, CT	261,938	23,568	+/-3,613	9.0%	+/-1.4%	370
Ocala, FL	329,035	64,222	+/-7,962	19.5%	+/-2.4%	83
Ocean City, NJ	94,252	8,835	+/-1,881	9.4%	+/-2.0%	365
Odessa, TX	147,095	21,501	+/-5,010	14.6%	+/-3.4%	265
Ogden-Clearfield, UT	615,823	64,161	+/-7,360	10.4%	+/-1.2%	356
Oklahoma City, OK	1,286,744	191,830	+/-11,090	14.9%	+/-0.9%	256
Olympia-Tumwater, WA	257,962	33,003	+/-5,603	12.8%	+/-2.2%	314
Omaha-Council Bluffs, NE-IA	878,790	111,619	+/-8,137	12.7%	+/-0.9%	317
Orlando-Kissimmee-Sanford, FL	2,221,209	380,933	+/-21,384	17.1%	+/-1.0%	151
Oshkosh-Neenah, WI	161,299	20,803	+/-2,586	12.9%	+/-1.6%	306
Owensboro, KY	114,097	18,450	+/-3,272	16.2%	+/-2.8%	198
Oxnard-Thousand Oaks-Ventura, CA	827,429	98,572	+/-8,115	11.9%	+/-1.0%	334
Palm Bay-Melbourne-Titusville, FL	545,062	81,662	+/-8,274	15.0%	+/-1.5%	252
Panama City, FL	186,734	33,000	+/-4,984	17.7%	+/-2.7%	132
Parkersburg-Vienna, WV	91,264	17,462	+/-2,480	19.1%	+/-2.7%	98
Pensacola-Ferry Pass-Brent, FL	439,944	70,881	+/-7,697	16.1%	+/-1.8%	203
Peoria, IL	372,862	47,768	+/-5,937	12.8%	+/-1.6%	312
Philadelphia-Camden-Wilmington, PA-NJ-DE-MD	5,884,173	792,981	+/-24,235	13.5%	+/-0.4%	296
Phoenix-Mesa-Scottsdale, AZ	4,325,550	760,706	+/-27,227	17.6%	+/-0.6%	137
Pine Bluff, AR	85,065	20,736	+/-3,415	24.4%	+/-3.8%	16
Pittsburgh, PA	2,300,779	294,363	+/-10,892	12.8%	+/-0.5%	313
Pittsfield, MA	123,230	15,214	+/-2,321	12.3%	+/-1.9%	326
Pocatello, ID	81,080	13,900	+/-2,892	17.1%	+/-3.5%	152

CRS-55

Metropolitan Area	Total Population	Number Poor		Poverty Rate (Percent Poor)		
		Estimate	Margin of Error[a]	Poverty Rate	Margin of Error[a]	Rank[b]
Port St. Lucie, FL	432,472	74,415	+/-8,455	17.2%	+/-1.9%	150
Portland-South Portland, ME	508,937	57,943	+/-5,961	11.4%	+/-1.2%	340
Portland-Vancouver-Hillsboro, OR-WA	2,281,296	308,138	+/-15,086	13.5%	+/-0.7%	295
Prescott, AZ	211,524	34,138	+/-5,228	16.1%	+/-2.5%	201
Providence-Warwick, RI-MA	1,546,498	221,286	+/-10,882	14.3%	+/-0.7%	279
Provo-Orem, UT	548,963	75,447	+/-6,089	13.7%	+/-1.1%	289
Pueblo, CO	156,624	31,544	+/-4,177	20.1%	+/-2.6%	68
Punta Gorda, FL	160,389	22,628	+/-3,501	14.1%	+/-2.2%	283
Racine, WI	190,473	24,323	+/-3,718	12.8%	+/-1.9%	315
Raleigh, NC	1,185,900	142,633	+/-10,445	12.0%	+/-0.9%	331
Rapid City, SD	137,575	19,947	+/-2,955	14.5%	+/-2.2%	271
Reading, PA	399,792	57,698	+/-6,204	14.4%	+/-1.5%	275
Redding, CA	176,419	35,501	+/-4,281	20.1%	+/-2.4%	69
Reno, NV	432,828	64,933	+/-5,926	15.0%	+/-1.4%	250
Richmond, VA	1,207,277	167,791	+/-9,831	13.9%	+/-0.8%	286
Riverside-San Bernardino-Ontario, CA	4,298,913	781,792	+/-23,534	18.2%	+/-0.5%	120
Roanoke, VA	303,618	43,633	+/-5,158	14.4%	+/-1.7%	276
Rochester, MN	208,650	16,523	+/-2,572	7.9%	+/-1.2%	377
Rochester, NY	1,042,829	153,728	+/-9,277	14.7%	+/-0.9%	264
Rockford, IL	339,554	52,494	+/-5,842	15.5%	+/-1.7%	233
Rocky Mount, NC	147,408	27,825	+/-3,839	18.9%	+/-2.6%	100
Rome, GA	91,478	20,423	+/-4,011	22.3%	+/-4.3%	32
Sacramento—Roseville—Arden-Arcade, CA	2,182,441	363,182	+/-16,433	16.6%	+/-0.8%	178
Saginaw, MI	190,729	34,020	+/-4,382	17.8%	+/-2.3%	127
Salem, OR	387,689	75,096	+/-8,212	19.4%	+/-2.1%	89
Sa inas, CA	409,021	73,031	+/-9,276	17.9%	+/-2.3%	126
Sa isbury, MD-DE	371,597	57,065	+/-6,429	15.4%	+/-1.7%	239
Salt Lake City, UT	1,124,872	139,442	+/-12,915	12.4%	+/-1.1%	323
San Angelo, TX	110,830	13,518	+/-3,197	12.2%	+/-2.9%	327
San Antonio-New Braunfels, TX	2,235,950	363,769	+/-18,299	16.3%	+/-0.8%	192
San Diego-Carlsbad, CA	3,129,334	475,773	+/-21,393	15.2%	+/-0.7%	243

Metropolitan Area	Total Population	Number Poor		Poverty Rate (Percent Poor)		
		Estimate	Margin of Error[a]	Poverty Rate	Margin of Error[a]	Rank[b]
San Francisco-Oakland-Hayward, CA	4,451,868	510,653	+/-18,671	11.5%	+/-0.4%	337
San Jose-Sunnyvale-Santa Clara, CA	1,891,182	198,842	+/-12,625	10.5%	+/-0.7%	352
San Luis Obispo-Paso Robles-Arroyo Grande, CA	260,653	39,910	+/-4,790	15.3%	+/-1.8%	240
Santa Cruz-Watsonville, CA	258,572	38,616	+/-5,176	14.9%	+/-2.0%	255
Santa Fe, NM	144,957	28,106	+/-3,669	19.4%	+/-2.5%	88
Santa Maria-Santa Barbara, CA	417,118	68,116	+/-7,119	16.3%	+/-1.7%	190
Santa Rosa, CA	489,398	60,812	+/-6,883	12.4%	+/-1.4%	321
Savannah, GA	353,391	61,227	+/-5,819	17.3%	+/-1.6%	147
Scranton—Wilkes-Barre—Hazleton, PA	540,307	83,819	+/-6,826	15.5%	+/-1.3%	230
Seattle-Tacoma-Bellevue, WA	3,555,501	446,327	+/-18,551	12.6%	+/-0.5%	319
Sebastian-Vero Beach, FL	140,482	18,836	+/-3,818	13.4%	+/-2.7%	298
Sebring, FL	96,247	18,094	+/-3,330	18.8%	+/-3.4%	105
Sheboygan, WI	111,769	12,842	+/-2,655	11.5%	+/-2.4%	336
Sherman-Denison, TX	119,767	20,052	+/-3,282	16.7%	+/-2.7%	174
Shreveport-Bossier City, LA	437,810	89,134	+/-7,782	20.4%	+/-1.8%	64
Sierra Vista-Douglas, AZ	116,375	22,254	+/-3,418	19.1%	+/-2.9%	99
Sioux City, IA-NE-SD	164,903	24,384	+/-3,514	14.8%	+/-2.2%	261
Sioux Falls, SD	237,869	21,361	+/-3,670	9.0%	+/-1.5%	371
South Bend-Mishawaka, IN-MI	306,908	61,584	+/-5,763	20.1%	+/-1.9%	70
Spartanburg, SC	310,176	58,165	+/-6,323	18.8%	+/-2.1%	107
Spokane-Spokane Valley, WA	518,992	87,011	+/-6,789	16.8%	+/-1.3%	173
Springfield, IL	207,477	32,420	+/-3,392	15.6%	+/-1.7%	225
Springfield, MA	590,986	99,343	+/-7,727	16.8%	+/-1.3%	171
Springfield, MO	435,561	81,533	+/-7,592	18.7%	+/-1.7%	108
Springfield, OH	132,887	24,653	+/-3,250	18.6%	+/-2.5%	114
St. Cloud, MN	183,531	24,877	+/-3,933	13.6%	+/-2.2%	293
St. George, UT	145,575	23,122	+/-4,312	15.9%	+/-3.0%	219
St. Joseph, MO-KS	119,933	18,614	+/-3,170	15.5%	+/-2.6%	229
St. Louis, MO-IL	2,740,729	352,550	+/-13,984	12.9%	+/-0.5%	309
State College, PA	139,046	27,490	+/-3,453	19.8%	+/-2.5%	79
Staunton-Waynesboro, VA	111,589	12,717	+/-2,542	11.4%	+/-2.2%	338

Metropolitan Area	Total Population	Number Poor		Poverty Rate (Percent Poor)		
		Estimate	Margin of Error[a]	Poverty Rate	Margin of Error[a]	Rank[b]
Stockton-Lodi, CA	690,366	137,663	+/-9,607	19.9%	+/-1.4%	73
Sumter, SC	105,762	21,047	+/-3,419	19.9%	+/-3.2%	74
Syracuse, NY	635,056	101,432	+/-7,069	16.0%	+/-1.1%	211
Tallahassee, FL	353,498	76,104	+/-5,983	21.5%	+/-1.7%	46
Tampa-St. Petersburg-Clearwater, FL	2,822,199	435,739	+/-20,238	15.4%	+/-0.7%	235
Terre Haute, IN	155,430	34,599	+/-4,388	22.3%	+/-2.7%	33
Texarkana, TX-AR	143,188	30,643	+/-4,351	21.4%	+/-2.9%	49
The Villages, FL	98,007	10,283	+/-2,179	10.5%	+/-2.2%	354
Toledo, OH	590,850	114,978	+/-7,622	19.5%	+/-1.3%	84
Topeka, KS	229,113	35,331	+/-4,404	15.4%	+/-1.9%	236
Trenton, NJ	352,368	41,667	+/-6,207	11.8%	+/-1.8%	335
Tucson, AZ	970,384	188,765	+/-11,845	19.5%	+/-1.2%	85
Tulsa, OK	945,445	139,947	+/-6,432	14.8%	+/-0.7%	259
Tuscaloosa, AL	224,068	38,697	+/-4,511	17.3%	+/-2.0%	149
Tyler, TX	211,205	35,817	+/-6,103	17.0%	+/-2.9%	162
Urban Honolulu, HI	951,718	89,684	+/-7,816	9.4%	+/-0.8%	363
Utica-Rome, NY	283,034	49,420	+/-4,952	17.5%	+/-1.7%	141
Valdosta, GA	139,018	37,443	+/-4,673	26.9%	+/-3.3%	9
Vallejo-Fairfield, CA	414,410	53,992	+/-6,058	13.0%	+/-1.5%	303
Victoria, TX	94,588	14,419	+/-3,427	15.2%	+/-3.6%	241
Vineland-Bridgeton, NJ	145,220	29,978	+/-4,515	20.6%	+/-3.1%	58
Virginia Beach-Norfolk-Newport News, VA-NC	1,636,396	212,866	+/-11,713	13.0%	+/-0.7%	304
Visalia-Porterville, CA	448,360	135,066	+/-9,722	30.1%	+/-2.2%	4
Waco, TX	246,267	52,469	+/-6,245	21.3%	+/-2.5%	51
Walla Walla, WA	57,958	10,668	+/-3,003	18.4%	+/-4.9%	115
Warner Robins, GA	180,041	28,665	+/-5,206	15.9%	+/-3.0%	216
Washington-Arlington-Alexandria, DC-VA-MD-WV	5,846,655	495,683	+/-19,944	8.5%	+/-0.3%	373
Waterloo-Cedar Falls, IA	161,729	24,304	+/-3,456	15.0%	+/-2.1%	248
Watertown-Fort Drum, NY	113,014	18,002	+/-3,646	15.9%	+/-3.2%	215
Wausau, WI	133,632	14,731	+/-2,808	11.0%	+/-2.1%	345
Weirton-Steubenville, WV-OH	120,609	19,551	+/-2,770	16.2%	+/-2.3%	196

Metropolitan Area	Total Population	Number Poor		Poverty Rate (Percent Poor)		
		Estimate	Margin of Error[a]	Poverty Rate	Margin of Error[a]	Rank[b]
Wenatchee, WA	112,492	16,636	+/-3,885	14.8%	+/-3.5%	260
Wheeling, WV-OH	138,642	21,491	+/-2,879	15.5%	+/-2.1%	231
Wichita Falls, TX	137,071	25,865	+/-3,446	18.9%	+/-2.4%	101
Wichita, KS	626,159	93,560	+/-7,251	14.9%	+/-1.2%	254
Williamsport, PA	110,934	14,991	+/-3,104	13.5%	+/-2.8%	294
Wilmington, NC	260,957	51,668	+/-6,726	19.8%	+/-2.5%	78
Winchester, VA-WV	124,642	8,432	+/-1,934	6.8%	+/-1.5%	380
Winston-Salem, NC	636,242	127,378	+/-10,165	20.0%	+/-1.6%	71
Worcester, MA-CT	895,779	119,575	+/-10,053	13.3%	+/-1.1%	301
Yakima, WA	243,340	50,581	+/-6,289	20.8%	+/-2.6%	55
York-Hanover, PA	428,323	47,161	+/-5,805	11.0%	+/-1.4%	347
Youngstown-Warren-Boardman, OH-PA	536,084	93,178	+/-6,320	17.4%	+/-1.2%	144
Yuba City, CA	166,398	31,142	+/-4,962	18.7%	+/-3.0%	109
Yuma, AZ	193,953	34,449	+/-4,738	17.8%	+/-2.4%	130

Source: Table prepared by the Congressional Research Service (CRS) based on U.S. Census Bureau 2013 American Community Survey (ACS) data, table series S1701: Poverty Status in the Past 12 Months, from the Census Bureau's American FactFinder, available on the Internet at http://factfinder2.census.gov/faces/nav/jsf/pages/index.xhtml.

a. Margin of error of an estimate based on a 90% statistical confidence level. When added to and subtracted from an estimate, the range reflects a 90% statistical confidence interval bounding the estimate.

b. Ranks are based on areas' poverty rate estimates for 2013. Because of sampling variability, an area's rank generally does not statistically differ from other areas with overlapping margins of error.

Appendix C. Poverty Estimates by Congressional District

Table C-1. Poverty by Congressional District: 2013

Congressional District	Total Population	Number Poor		Poverty Rate (Percent Poor)		
		Estimate	Margin of Error[a]	Estimate	Margin of Error[a]	Rank[b]
Alabama						
1st	680,039	134,336	+/-9,624	19.8%	1.4%	94
2nd	669,393	131,402	+/-8,126	19.6%	1.2%	97
3rd	677,175	134,678	+/-9,229	19.9%	1.3%	93
4th	676,562	118,192	+/-8,753	17.5%	1.3%	149
5th	684,710	108,037	+/-7,907	15.8%	1.1%	192
6th	684,445	78,856	+/-6,788	11.5%	1.0%	340
7th	643,781	177,870	+/-9,741	27.6%	1.5%	16
Alaska						
(at Large)	718,359	67,016	+/-4,778	9.3%	0.7%	388
Arizona						
1st	695,472	155,250	+/-8,082	22.3%	1.2%	58
2nd	693,316	118,822	+/-9,247	17.1%	1.3%	162
3rd	698,447	163,662	+/-11,048	23.4%	1.5%	46
4th	705,492	122,569	+/-12,447	17.4%	1.7%	156
5th	755,207	68,362	+/-7,732	9.1%	1.0%	391
6th	733,123	82,235	+/-8,134	11.2%	1.1%	348
7th	740,117	273,768	+/-16,029	37.0%	1.9%	3
8th	729,202	81,101	+/-10,398	11.1%	1.4%	354
9th	726,815	140,691	+/-12,946	19.4%	1.7%	103
Arkansas						
1st	700,752	151,217	+/-9,195	21.6%	1.3%	64
2nd	735,135	115,908	+/-10,118	15.8%	1.4%	193
3rd	739,766	140,429	+/-10,887	19.0%	1.5%	113
4th	697,687	157,915	+/-8,674	22.6%	1.2%	53

Congressional District	Total Population	Number Poor		Poverty Rate (Percent Poor)		
		Estimate	Margin of Error[a]	Estimate	Margin of Error[a]	Rank[b]
California						
1st	686,482	127,948	+/-7,972	18.6%	1.1%	123
2nd	698,111	95,297	+/-7,216	13.7%	1.0%	267
3rd	692,439	113,156	+/-9,888	16.3%	1.4%	181
4th	691,590	76,856	+/-8,030	11.1%	1.2%	354
5th	704,754	91,858	+/-7,901	13.0%	1.1%	291
6th	720,620	173,402	+/-12,209	24.1%	1.6%	41
7th	710,789	98,887	+/-10,134	13.9%	1.4%	258
8th	693,599	151,099	+/-9,870	21.8%	1.4%	62
9th	713,742	141,208	+/-11,730	19.8%	1.6%	94
10th	710,043	135,348	+/-10,141	19.1%	1.4%	111
11th	725,609	86,409	+/-8,468	11.9%	1.1%	326
12th	724,204	100,585	+/-7,012	13.9%	1.0%	258
13th	715,115	127,993	+/-9,097	17.9%	1.3%	139
14th	713,923	59,242	+/-6,449	8.3%	0.9%	402
15th	724,469	63,947	+/-7,598	8.8%	1.0%	397
16th	695,284	228,299	+/-14,216	32.8%	1.8%	5
17th	723,712	54,067	+/-5,872	7.5%	0.8%	416
18th	718,830	52,354	+/-7,304	7.3%	1.0%	419
19th	736,944	106,113	+/-9,730	14.4%	1.3%	241
20th	693,918	121,640	+/-11,271	17.5%	1.6%	150
21st	666,828	198,925	+/-13,312	29.8%	1.9%	9
22nd	721,442	162,392	+/-13,227	22.5%	1.7%	57
23rd	705,535	139,601	+/-12,652	19.8%	1.7%	94
24th	687,555	108,598	+/-9,062	15.8%	1.3%	193
25th	703,152	98,322	+/-10,491	14.0%	1.4%	255
26th	701,251	91,980	+/-7,814	13.1%	1.1%	288
27th	705,546	97,711	+/-8,203	13.8%	1.2%	263
28th	702,945	116,658	+/-7,486	16.6%	1.0%	174
29th	686,505	154,924	+/-11,036	22.6%	1.4%	53
30th	736,172	101,938	+/-8,322	13.8%	1.1%	263
31st	704,960	149,510	+/-11,708	21.2%	1.6%	70
32nd	695,234	111,294	+/-10,142	16.0%	1.4%	190
33rd	699,130	71,356	+/-8,189	10.2%	1.1%	375
34th	694,761	204,453	+/-11,977	29.4%	1.5%	10

Congressional District	Total Population	Number Poor		Poverty Rate (Percent Poor)		
		Estimate	Margin of Error[a]	Estimate	Margin of Error[a]	Rank[b]
35th	712,143	123,251	+/-10,376	17.3%	1.4%	158
36th	710,157	150,803	+/-12,089	21.2%	1.7%	70
37th	721,328	150,105	+/-9,344	20.8%	1.1%	78
38th	716,149	91,962	+/-8,974	12.8%	1.2%	299
39th	713,500	79,713	+/-8,186	11.2%	1.1%	348
40th	713,330	208,796	+/-13,307	29.3%	1.6%	12
41st	721,684	145,863	+/-11,526	20.2%	1.6%	85
42nd	737,375	88,252	+/-11,066	12.0%	1.5%	323
43rd	721,992	154,696	+/-12,164	21.4%	1.6%	67
44th	697,779	169,473	+/-13,325	24.3%	1.7%	39
45th	724,246	59,876	+/-6,525	8.3%	0.9%	402
46th	708,339	147,887	+/-11,656	20.9%	1.6%	75
47th	714,775	127,302	+/-9,765	17.8%	1.4%	145
48th	720,127	81,814	+/-8,059	11.4%	1.1%	343
49th	699,611	87,453	+/-8,497	12.5%	1.2%	306
50th	722,543	96,900	+/-10,044	13.4%	1.3%	282
51st	710,971	175,732	+/-13,156	24.7%	1.7%	37
52nd	690,588	72,736	+/-6,238	10.5%	0.9%	372
53rd	731,261	102,840	+/-12,694	14.1%	1.6%	252

Colorado

1st	759,232	128,553	+/-9,726	16.9%	1.3%	168
2nd	735,914	86,969	+/-6,347	11.8%	0.8%	330
3rd	704,491	114,613	+/-8,093	16.3%	1.1%	181
4th	730,209	81,105	+/-7,648	11.1%	1.1%	354
5th	719,869	80,961	+/-7,616	11.2%	1.1%	348
6th	758,469	88,906	+/-7,620	11.7%	1.0%	335
7th	743,277	86,339	+/-8,100	11.6%	1.1%	336

Connecticut

1st	701,540	87,123	+/-7,184	12.4%	1.0%	310
2nd	673,205	57,137	+/-5,536	8.5%	0.8%	400
3rd	692,492	82,119	+/-8,301	11.9%	1.2%	326
4th	722,098	72,043	+/-6,567	10.0%	0.9%	378
5th	696,018	75,478	+/-8,848	10.8%	1.3%	365

Congressional District	Total Population	Number Poor		Poverty Rate (Percent Poor)		
		Estimate	Margin of Error[a]	Estimate	Margin of Error[a]	Rank[b]
Delaware						
(at Large)	900,322	111,327	+/-9,589	12.4%	1.1%	310
District of Columbia						
Delegate District (at Large)	611,788	115,551	+/-7,400	18.9%	1.2%	116
Florida						
1st	695,249	111,431	+/-9,748	16.0%	1.4%	190
2nd	664,146	138,714	+/-8,918	20.9%	1.3%	75
3rd	667,485	124,771	+/-8,585	18.7%	1.2%	120
4th	689,505	84,028	+/-7,680	12.2%	1.1%	315
5th	711,039	198,766	+/-12,906	28.0%	1.7%	15
6th	708,733	106,156	+/-8,431	15.0%	1.2%	224
7th	692,433	94,550	+/-9,495	13.7%	1.4%	267
8th	696,381	103,069	+/-9,922	14.8%	1.4%	229
9th	760,571	156,829	+/-15,275	20.6%	1.9%	82
10th	722,655	97,486	+/-10,462	13.5%	1.4%	277
11th	693,689	112,549	+/-10,734	16.2%	1.5%	185
12th	708,043	81,956	+/-6,680	11.6%	0.9%	336
13th	686,676	101,749	+/-10,216	14.8%	1.4%	229
14th	721,858	157,423	+/-12,447	21.8%	1.7%	62
15th	702,978	104,517	+/-10,034	14.9%	1.3%	227
16th	717,345	103,612	+/-8,227	14.4%	1.2%	241
17th	698,886	126,399	+/-10,568	18.1%	1.5%	133
18th	698,549	94,808	+/-9,038	13.6%	1.4%	270
19th	724,927	108,843	+/-8,829	15.0%	1.2%	224
20th	713,673	170,473	+/-12,666	23.9%	1.7%	44
21st	735,327	82,380	+/-7,434	11.2%	1.0%	348
22nd	725,143	110,474	+/-9,617	15.2%	1.3%	212
23rd	715,782	98,480	+/-9,106	13.8%	1.3%	263
24th	710,949	176,066	+/-11,881	24.8%	1.5%	34
25th	730,690	134,139	+/-12,580	18.4%	1.7%	125
26th	727,003	130,805	+/-11,568	18.0%	1.6%	135

Congressional District	Total Population	Number Poor		Poverty Rate (Percent Poor)		
		Estimate	Margin of Error[a]	Estimate	Margin of Error[a]	Rank[b]
27th	710,235	142,860	+/-10,599	20.1%	1.5%	90
Georgia						
1st	696,283	135,297	+/-8,201	19.4%	1.2%	103
2nd	651,114	177,017	+/-10,143	27.2%	1.5%	21
3rd	698,416	114,099	+/-10,317	16.3%	1.4%	181
4th	713,620	130,139	+/-10,983	18.2%	1.4%	131
5th	681,675	171,956	+/-10,676	25.2%	1.5%	32
6th	723,162	77,563	+/-8,599	10.7%	1.1%	369
7th	727,932	89,058	+/-11,176	12.2%	1.5%	315
8th	671,524	145,324	+/-9,494	21.6%	1.4%	64
9th	698,289	140,702	+/-9,000	20.1%	1.3%	90
10th	675,678	131,630	+/-9,051	19.5%	1.4%	100
11th	718,088	100,655	+/-9,127	14.0%	1.2%	255
12th	672,726	167,385	+/-9,407	24.9%	1.4%	33
13th	711,290	131,182	+/-12,045	18.4%	1.6%	125
14th	681,117	131,761	+/-11,132	19.3%	1.6%	105
Hawaii						
1st	682,599	60,920	+/-5,936	8.9%	0.9%	395
2nd	685,063	87,448	+/-8,573	12.8%	1.2%	299
Idaho						
1st	794,263	123,653	+/-11,335	15.6%	1.4%	197
2nd	788,648	122,897	+/-8,979	15.6%	1.1%	197
Illinois						
1st	706,988	142,867	+/-10,464	20.2%	1.3%	85
2nd	688,548	156,163	+/-11,550	22.7%	1.5%	52
3rd	726,153	95,484	+/-10,108	13.1%	1.3%	288
4th	706,214	159,724	+/-13,235	22.6%	1.8%	53
5th	724,010	77,359	+/-7,300	10.7%	1.0%	369
6th	718,055	37,073	+/-4,607	5.2%	0.6%	434
7th	694,980	178,591	+/-11,471	25.7%	1.4%	30
8th	708,838	78,817	+/-9,914	11.1%	1.3%	354

Congressional District	Total Population	Number Poor		Poverty Rate (Percent Poor)		
		Estimate	Margin of Error[a]	Estimate	Margin of Error[a]	Rank[b]
9th	690,182	88,569	+/-10,431	12.8%	1.4%	299
10th	697,471	68,938	+/-8,091	9.9%	1.2%	379
11th	702,136	72,337	+/-8,170	10.3%	1.2%	374
12th	680,740	124,967	+/-8,488	18.4%	1.2%	125
13th	671,586	126,612	+/-6,875	18.9%	1.0%	116
14th	723,626	46,575	+/-6,539	6.4%	0.9%	427
15th	678,016	102,470	+/-6,889	15.1%	1.0%	216
16th	675,968	88,029	+/-7,114	13.0%	1.0%	291
17th	687,108	125,847	+/-7,516	18.3%	1.1%	129
18th	696,061	74,971	+/-6,694	10.8%	0.9%	365
Indiana						
1st	700,997	116,370	+/-8,928	16.6%	1.3%	174
2nd	696,539	127,392	+/-9,910	18.3%	1.4%	129
3rd	714,127	109,110	+/-7,422	15.3%	1.0%	208
4th	706,708	88,829	+/-6,945	12.6%	1.0%	302
5th	725,857	80,839	+/-6,625	11.1%	0.9%	354
6th	701,236	107,593	+/-6,591	15.3%	0.9%	208
7th	724,464	174,561	+/-9,964	24.1%	1.4%	41
8th	689,998	103,928	+/-7,111	15.1%	1.0%	216
9th	707,964	106,505	+/-6,825	15.0%	0.9%	224
Iowa						
1st	740,372	87,534	+/-6,449	11.8%	0.9%	330
2nd	747,690	103,748	+/-6,748	13.9%	0.9%	258
3rd	771,820	89,857	+/-6,573	11.6%	0.9%	336
4th	731,788	97,988	+/-5,435	13.4%	0.7%	282
Kansas						
1st	693,632	107,739	+/-7,630	15.5%	1.1%	203
2nd	686,122	105,331	+/-7,651	15.4%	1.1%	206
3rd	730,158	73,746	+/-6,487	10.1%	0.9%	377
4th	701,810	106,542	+/-7,729	15.2%	1.1%	212

Congressional District	Total Population	Number Poor		Poverty Rate (Percent Poor)		
		Estimate	Margin of Error[a]	Estimate	Margin of Error[a]	Rank[b]
Kentucky						
1st	697,666	141,016	+/-8,612	20.2%	1.2%	85
2nd	715,427	122,473	+/-7,098	17.1%	1.0%	162
3rd	724,794	116,814	+/-9,917	16.1%	1.4%	187
4th	718,449	101,001	+/-7,858	14.1%	1.1%	252
5th	690,896	184,181	+/-7,867	26.7%	1.1%	24
6th	719,324	135,150	+/-9,981	18.8%	1.4%	118
Louisiana						
1st	766,678	103,791	+/-7,676	13.5%	1.0%	277
2nd	766,962	203,181	+/-11,910	26.5%	1.4%	26
3rd	753,214	125,639	+/-10,136	16.7%	1.3%	173
4th	739,473	157,598	+/-9,017	21.3%	1.2%	69
5th	706,617	175,044	+/-9,880	24.8%	1.4%	34
6th	762,045	122,766	+/-11,353	16.1%	1.4%	187
Maine						
1st	655,033	78,463	+/-7,100	12.0%	1.1%	323
2nd	638,794	102,176	+/-6,263	16.0%	1.0%	190
Maryland						
1st	706,758	75,818	+/-6,510	10.7%	0.9%	369
2nd	726,237	86,928	+/-7,834	12.0%	1.0%	323
3rd	722,483	57,302	+/-5,320	7.9%	0.7%	410
4th	733,322	66,977	+/-7,518	9.1%	1.0%	391
5th	729,944	55,364	+/-6,138	7.6%	0.9%	415
6th	724,866	70,066	+/-7,963	9.7%	1.1%	381
7th	699,540	123,371	+/-9,075	17.6%	1.2%	148
8th	745,009	49,745	+/-5,484	6.7%	0.7%	423
Massachusetts						
1st	705,884	110,719	+/-8,093	15.7%	1.1%	196
2nd	700,887	97,862	+/-9,167	14.0%	1.3%	255
3rd	723,728	88,513	+/-7,272	12.2%	1.0%	315
4th	720,531	53,523	+/-6,566	7.4%	0.9%	417

Congressional District	Total Population	Number Poor		Poverty Rate (Percent Poor)		
		Estimate	Margin of Error[a]	Estimate	Margin of Error[a]	Rank[b]
5th	726,369	59,426	+/-6,659	8.2%	0.9%	404
6th	733,179	64,388	+/-7,237	8.8%	1.0%	397
7th	700,909	147,321	+/-8,826	21.0%	1.2%	73
8th	742,643	68,341	+/-6,059	9.2%	0.8%	389
9th	702,400	80,420	+/-6,601	11.4%	0.9%	343
Michigan						
1st	677,511	105,897	+/-6,121	15.6%	0.9%	197
2nd	697,928	108,808	+/-8,067	15.6%	1.1%	197
3rd	702,211	104,450	+/-8,143	14.9%	1.2%	227
4th	680,380	125,254	+/-7,395	18.4%	1.1%	125
5th	672,090	143,625	+/-9,525	21.4%	1.4%	67
6th	692,828	116,451	+/-7,098	16.8%	1.0%	171
7th	677,666	98,989	+/-7,538	14.6%	1.1%	237
8th	693,631	84,016	+/-7,169	12.1%	1.0%	319
9th	706,738	104,802	+/-8,448	14.8%	1.1%	229
10th	702,803	81,835	+/-7,088	11.6%	1.0%	336
11th	712,460	47,489	+/-5,567	6.7%	0.8%	423
12th	692,599	124,184	+/-8,814	17.9%	1.2%	139
13th	665,000	218,929	+/-10,358	32.9%	1.5%	4
14th	695,668	183,707	+/-10,674	26.4%	1.4%	27
Minnesota						
1st	646,253	74,282	+/-5,790	11.5%	0.9%	341
2nd	669,895	56,383	+/-6,891	8.4%	1.0%	401
3rd	679,780	43,492	+/-6,880	6.4%	1.0%	427
4th	668,045	90,824	+/-6,299	13.6%	0.9%	270
5th	677,566	113,609	+/-9,034	16.8%	1.3%	171
6th	661,749	54,232	+/-5,275	8.2%	0.8%	404
7th	644,866	76,505	+/-4,410	11.9%	0.7%	326
8th	644,194	83,095	+/-4,924	12.9%	0.8%	296
Mississippi						
1st	737,103	152,530	+/-10,500	20.7%	1.4%	80
2nd	696,410	226,515	+/-10,737	32.5%	1.5%	6

Congressional District	Total Population	Number Poor		Poverty Rate (Percent Poor)		
		Estimate	Margin of Error[a]	Estimate	Margin of Error[a]	Rank[b]
3rd	722,227	160,723	+/-10,624	22.3%	1.5%	58
4th	738,028	156,147	+/-11,579	21.2%	1.6%	70
Missouri						
1st	716,639	154,322	+/-10,183	21.5%	1.4%	66
2nd	756,366	44,541	+/-6,446	5.9%	0.8%	430
3rd	740,733	83,265	+/-7,766	11.2%	1.0%	348
4th	718,835	141,025	+/-7,822	19.6%	1.1%	98
5th	746,309	134,121	+/-8,703	18.0%	1.1%	135
6th	723,996	96,173	+/-7,357	13.3%	1.0%	286
7th	737,825	131,801	+/-7,212	17.9%	1.0%	139
8th	720,306	145,818	+/-9,106	20.2%	1.3%	85
Montana						
(at Large)	990,603	163,637	+/-9,336	16.5%	0.9%	176
Nebraska						
1st	608,570	78,276	+/-7,294	12.9%	1.2%	296
2nd	622,083	84,591	+/-6,643	13.6%	1.1%	270
3rd	584,912	76,566	+/-6,430	13.1%	1.1%	288
Nevada						
1st	664,608	150,284	+/-10,320	22.6%	1.6%	53
2nd	678,429	96,988	+/-7,124	14.3%	1.0%	246
3rd	716,933	69,515	+/-7,275	9.7%	1.1%	381
4th	690,506	116,789	+/-11,216	16.9%	1.5%	168
New Hampshire						
1st	642,184	50,458	+/-5,547	7.9%	0.9%	410
2nd	638,997	61,037	+/-6,572	9.6%	1.0%	384
New Jersey						
1st	719,415	97,145	+/-8,049	13.5%	1.1%	277
2nd	711,019	111,174	+/-8,251	15.6%	1.1%	197
3rd	726,173	39,334	+/-4,382	5.4%	0.6%	433

Congressional District	Total Population	Number Poor		Poverty Rate (Percent Poor)		
		Estimate	Margin of Error[a]	Estimate	Margin of Error[a]	Rank[b]
4th	726,617	69,746	+/-7,488	9.6%	1.1%	384
5th	719,355	50,882	+/-6,204	7.1%	0.9%	421
6th	712,290	84,373	+/-8,494	11.8%	1.2%	330
7th	735,736	35,040	+/-5,067	4.8%	0.7%	435
8th	751,289	144,504	+/-10,611	19.2%	1.4%	108
9th	755,519	113,758	+/-8,908	15.1%	1.2%	216
10th	714,062	148,640	+/-9,667	20.8%	1.3%	78
11th	721,415	33,693	+/-5,311	4.7%	0.7%	436
12th	728,120	70,260	+/-7,796	9.6%	1.1%	384
New Mexico						
1st	685,428	133,437	+/-9,937	19.5%	1.4%	100
2nd	676,488	154,795	+/-8,582	22.9%	1.2%	51
3rd	683,486	160,229	+/-9,712	23.4%	1.4%	46
New York						
1st	701,326	49,336	+/-5,985	7.0%	0.9%	422
2nd	712,372	46,878	+/-6,011	6.6%	0.8%	425
3rd	712,917	38,868	+/-5,395	5.5%	0.8%	432
4th	702,715	50,575	+/-6,569	7.2%	0.9%	420
5th	756,885	110,838	+/-9,391	14.6%	1.2%	237
6th	713,917	96,359	+/-9,486	13.5%	1.3%	277
7th	751,238	200,749	+/-13,007	26.7%	1.6%	24
8th	729,789	180,209	+/-12,403	24.7%	1.5%	37
9th	731,047	146,945	+/-9,562	20.1%	1.2%	90
10th	698,689	118,623	+/-11,829	17.0%	1.5%	166
11th	721,525	99,117	+/-8,696	13.7%	1.2%	267
12th	700,886	87,458	+/-7,326	12.5%	1.1%	306
13th	753,771	231,790	+/-14,629	30.8%	1.8%	7
14th	708,751	132,359	+/-10,918	18.7%	1.4%	120
15th	734,051	292,239	+/-13,036	39.8%	1.5%	2
16th	716,038	92,855	+/-8,224	13.0%	1.1%	291
17th	722,094	81,843	+/-8,290	11.3%	1.2%	346
18th	694,344	72,932	+/-6,695	10.5%	1.0%	372
19th	678,168	84,606	+/-7,505	12.5%	1.1%	306

Congressional District	Total Population	Number Poor		Poverty Rate (Percent Poor)		
		Estimate	Margin of Error[a]	Estimate	Margin of Error[a]	Rank[b]
20th	695,685	94,550	+/-7,852	13.6%	1.1%	270
21st	674,976	102,053	+/-7,404	15.1%	1.1%	216
22nd	678,127	111,998	+/-7,800	16.5%	1.1%	176
23rd	671,906	114,125	+/-7,004	17.0%	1.0%	166
24th	688,710	103,904	+/-6,705	15.1%	1.0%	216
25th	698,713	112,337	+/-7,799	16.1%	1.1%	187
26th	696,725	134,322	+/-7,785	19.3%	1.1%	105
27th	688,608	67,777	+/-5,673	9.8%	0.8%	380
North Carolina						
1st	691,089	185,667	+/-10,290	26.9%	1.4%	23
2nd	760,912	122,942	+/-9,604	16.2%	1.2%	185
3rd	715,163	123,544	+/-8,781	17.3%	1.2%	158
4th	733,092	133,671	+/-10,387	18.2%	1.3%	131
5th	726,793	137,941	+/-8,718	19.0%	1.1%	113
6th	742,799	111,853	+/-9,124	15.1%	1.2%	216
7th	750,313	144,958	+/-7,926	19.3%	1.0%	105
8th	726,125	148,570	+/-9,452	20.5%	1.3%	84
9th	774,136	61,437	+/-6,755	7.9%	0.9%	410
10th	725,747	128,534	+/-8,986	17.7%	1.2%	147
11th	720,043	136,702	+/-9,351	19.0%	1.3%	113
12th	746,929	204,194	+/-11,575	27.3%	1.4%	19
13th	775,136	75,384	+/-9,217	9.7%	1.2%	381
North Dakota						
(at Large)	698,199	82,398	+/-5,117	11.8%	0.7%	330
Ohio						
1st	702,707	125,501	+/-8,795	17.9%	1.3%	139
2nd	714,389	110,534	+/-8,590	15.5%	1.2%	203
3rd	717,654	167,292	+/-10,487	23.3%	1.4%	48
4th	679,889	91,334	+/-7,236	13.4%	1.1%	282
5th	710,347	89,156	+/-7,234	12.6%	1.0%	302
6th	689,436	123,434	+/-7,424	17.9%	1.0%	139
7th	703,754	91,533	+/-7,137	13.0%	1.0%	291

Congressional District	Total Population	Number Poor		Poverty Rate (Percent Poor)		
		Estimate	Margin of Error[a]	Estimate	Margin of Error[a]	Rank[b]
8th	703,535	97,089	+/-8,397	13.8%	1.2%	263
9th	700,743	155,919	+/-9,614	22.3%	1.3%	58
10th	698,963	122,937	+/-8,690	17.6%	1.2%	148
11th	672,657	185,770	+/-8,488	27.6%	1.2%	16
12th	724,734	80,548	+/-8,542	11.1%	1.1%	354
13th	697,304	137,989	+/-8,203	19.8%	1.1%	94
14th	714,373	64,344	+/-6,724	9.0%	0.9%	394
15th	709,268	95,574	+/-9,204	13.5%	1.2%	277
16th	709,000	57,988	+/-7,104	8.2%	1.0%	404
Oklahoma						
1st	761,062	116,136	+/-6,147	15.3%	0.8%	208
2nd	722,939	148,957	+/-6,518	20.6%	0.9%	82
3rd	737,954	105,777	+/-6,092	14.3%	0.8%	246
4th	747,633	113,007	+/-6,680	15.1%	0.9%	216
5th	765,619	143,029	+/-8,923	18.7%	1.1%	120
Oregon						
1st	784,374	88,715	+/-8,193	11.3%	1.0%	346
2nd	761,782	137,247	+/-10,784	18.0%	1.4%	135
3rd	781,957	140,701	+/-9,197	18.0%	1.2%	135
4th	755,543	157,618	+/-9,833	20.9%	1.3%	75
5th	769,215	117,857	+/-9,483	15.3%	1.2%	208
Pennsylvania						
1st	708,585	179,930	+/-12,234	25.4%	1.6%	31
2nd	679,969	187,309	+/-12,997	27.5%	1.7%	18
3rd	675,518	96,849	+/-6,914	14.3%	1.0%	246
4th	686,631	75,245	+/-7,028	11.0%	1.0%	362
5th	653,380	106,830	+/-6,726	16.4%	1.0%	180
6th	702,677	54,490	+/-5,690	7.8%	0.8%	413
7th	698,765	38,806	+/-5,427	5.6%	0.8%	431
8th	699,630	42,426	+/-5,300	6.1%	0.8%	429
9th	677,732	105,526	+/-6,659	15.6%	1.0%	197
10th	677,709	78,320	+/-6,295	11.6%	0.9%	336

Congressional District	Total Population	Number Poor		Poverty Rate (Percent Poor)		
		Estimate	Margin of Error[a]	Estimate	Margin of Error[a]	Rank[b]
11th	678,516	87,815	+/-7,528	12.9%	1.1%	296
12th	689,855	66,446	+/-5,751	9.6%	0.8%	384
13th	699,764	94,833	+/-9,401	13.6%	1.3%	270
14th	677,236	129,813	+/-6,629	19.2%	1.0%	108
15th	690,532	83,356	+/-7,214	12.1%	1.0%	319
16th	691,003	99,925	+/-7,985	14.5%	1.1%	239
17th	673,191	99,143	+/-7,599	14.7%	1.1%	235
18th	692,563	63,343	+/-6,733	9.1%	1.0%	391
Puerto Rico						
Resident Commissioner District (at Large)	3,581,841	1,626,879	+/-25,081	45.4%	0.7%	1
Rhode Island						
1st	507,705	83,640	+/-7,475	16.5%	1.4%	176
2nd	503,122	60,806	+/-6,404	12.1%	1.2%	319
South Carolina						
1st	702,942	93,237	+/-8,472	13.3%	1.2%	286
2nd	652,110	88,521	+/-7,452	13.6%	1.1%	270
3rd	640,182	122,644	+/-8,617	19.2%	1.4%	108
4th	672,211	117,654	+/-11,317	17.5%	1.7%	150
5th	665,846	116,437	+/-8,915	17.5%	1.3%	150
6th	635,209	173,720	+/-12,202	27.3%	1.8%	19
7th	663,301	148,167	+/-9,307	22.3%	1.4%	58
South Dakota						
(at Large)	815,049	115,454	+/-6,396	14.2%	0.8%	249
Tennessee						
1st	691,578	134,589	+/-8,688	19.5%	1.3%	100
2nd	704,547	115,039	+/-8,035	16.3%	1.1%	181
3rd	704,206	130,627	+/-8,498	18.5%	1.2%	124
4th	708,757	109,876	+/-9,823	15.5%	1.4%	203
5th	717,954	125,063	+/-10,508	17.4%	1.5%	156

Congressional District	Total Population	Number Poor		Poverty Rate (Percent Poor)		
		Estimate	Margin of Error[a]	Estimate	Margin of Error[a]	Rank[b]
6th	711,308	117,565	+/-8,039	16.5%	1.1%	176
7th	710,702	105,314	+/-7,598	14.8%	1.1%	229
8th	690,620	99,693	+/-7,837	14.4%	1.1%	241
9th	695,623	189,006	+/-10,197	27.2%	1.4%	21
Texas						
1st	687,535	131,109	+/-9,739	19.1%	1.4%	111
2nd	713,206	77,574	+/-9,226	10.9%	1.3%	363
3rd	761,975	61,299	+/-7,654	8.0%	1.0%	407
4th	692,508	116,697	+/-7,652	16.9%	1.1%	168
5th	702,251	121,143	+/-9,754	17.3%	1.4%	158
6th	723,550	98,531	+/-9,801	13.6%	1.3%	270
7th	739,161	95,951	+/-12,599	13.0%	1.6%	291
8th	723,034	106,875	+/-12,178	14.8%	1.7%	229
9th	732,651	170,582	+/-15,618	23.3%	1.9%	48
10th	743,786	93,471	+/-9,733	12.6%	1.3%	302
11th	707,102	100,293	+/-8,202	14.2%	1.1%	249
12th	715,352	90,096	+/-9,395	12.6%	1.2%	302
13th	666,624	113,891	+/-7,896	17.1%	1.2%	162
14th	685,799	120,238	+/-10,196	17.5%	1.5%	150
15th	712,583	206,766	+/-14,700	29.0%	1.9%	13
16th	713,506	149,716	+/-11,335	21.0%	1.6%	73
17th	697,313	144,209	+/-9,217	20.7%	1.3%	80
18th	719,940	174,321	+/-12,611	24.2%	1.6%	40
19th	676,937	118,302	+/-7,916	17.5%	1.2%	150
20th	738,710	149,099	+/-11,527	20.2%	1.5%	85
21st	725,911	89,810	+/-8,990	12.4%	1.2%	310
22nd	776,804	62,068	+/-8,980	8.0%	1.1%	407
23rd	704,310	132,124	+/-12,368	18.8%	1.6%	118
24th	737,662	81,517	+/-7,194	11.1%	1.0%	354
25th	698,238	84,487	+/-7,903	12.1%	1.1%	319
26th	754,463	60,365	+/-7,755	8.0%	1.0%	407
27th	700,545	121,425	+/-7,765	17.3%	1.1%	158
28th	716,462	185,834	+/-13,454	25.9%	1.8%	29
29th	725,214	205,537	+/-15,022	28.3%	1.9%	14

Congressional District	Total Population	Number Poor		Poverty Rate (Percent Poor)		
		Estimate	Margin of Error[a]	Estimate	Margin of Error[a]	Rank[b]
30th	730,093	181,102	+/-12,840	24.8%	1.7%	34
31st	755,146	81,363	+/-8,607	10.8%	1.1%	365
32nd	712,450	102,395	+/-10,552	14.4%	1.4%	241
33rd	718,202	211,105	+/-14,105	29.4%	1.7%	10
34th	699,377	214,124	+/-14,414	30.6%	1.9%	8
35th	734,454	176,578	+/-13,103	24.0%	1.6%	43
36th	691,375	100,042	+/-9,328	14.5%	1.3%	239
Utah						
1st	710,878	79,725	+/-6,787	11.2%	0.9%	348
2nd	701,563	99,573	+/-8,257	14.2%	1.1%	249
3rd	703,653	94,122	+/-6,866	13.4%	1.0%	282
4th	735,493	87,761	+/-9,686	11.9%	1.3%	326
Vermont						
(at Large)	602,538	74,058	+/-5,273	12.3%	0.9%	313
Virginia						
1st	744,218	66,370	+/-8,115	8.9%	1.1%	395
2nd	702,902	75,806	+/-7,226	10.8%	1.0%	365
3rd	713,004	169,763	+/-8,239	23.8%	1.2%	45
4th	706,932	88,229	+/-8,412	12.5%	1.2%	306
5th	705,461	106,670	+/-7,457	15.1%	1.0%	216
6th	698,956	106,450	+/-8,106	15.2%	1.2%	212
7th	746,510	55,579	+/-5,781	7.4%	0.8%	417
8th	768,254	59,318	+/-7,803	7.7%	1.0%	414
9th	691,431	125,424	+/-7,101	18.1%	1.0%	133
10th	775,923	35,554	+/-5,723	4.6%	0.7%	437
11th	756,953	49,570	+/-6,419	6.5%	0.8%	426
Washington						
1st	701,188	64,725	+/-7,748	9.2%	1.1%	389
2nd	679,236	98,032	+/-9,375	14.4%	1.4%	241
3rd	684,902	95,133	+/-7,202	13.9%	1.0%	258
4th	688,694	123,122	+/-10,455	17.9%	1.5%	139

Congressional District	Total Population	Number Poor		Poverty Rate (Percent Poor)		
		Estimate	Margin of Error[a]	Estimate	Margin of Error[a]	Rank[b]
5th	652,983	116,228	+/-7,411	17.8%	1.1%	145
6th	661,196	97,169	+/-8,145	14.7%	1.2%	235
7th	689,597	84,405	+/-6,843	12.2%	1.0%	315
8th	694,338	79,365	+/-8,803	11.4%	1.2%	343
9th	697,715	107,630	+/-9,397	15.4%	1.3%	206
10th	686,413	101,473	+/-9,503	14.8%	1.3%	229
West Virginia						
1st	593,790	101,747	+/-6,634	17.1%	1.1%	162
2nd	613,973	93,591	+/-6,940	15.2%	1.1%	212
3rd	590,503	137,009	+/-8,296	23.2%	1.4%	50
Wisconsin						
1st	693,828	81,867	+/-7,526	11.8%	1.1%	330
2nd	716,614	100,772	+/-7,885	14.1%	1.1%	252
3rd	680,168	94,351	+/-5,668	13.9%	0.8%	258
4th	697,611	182,145	+/-7,715	26.1%	1.1%	28
5th	709,150	62,002	+/-5,486	8.7%	0.8%	399
6th	689,717	70,099	+/-4,808	10.2%	0.7%	375
7th	701,635	86,042	+/-5,816	12.3%	0.8%	313
8th	704,474	78,273	+/-5,835	11.1%	0.8%	354
Wyoming						
(at Large)	569,307	62,039	+/-5,844	10.9%	1.0%	363

Source: Table prepared by the Congressional Research Service (CRS) based on analysis of U.S. Census Bureau 2013 American Community Survey (ACS) data, table series S1701: Poverty Status in the Past 12 Months, from the Census Bureau's American FactFinder, available on the Internet at http://factfinder2.census.gov/faces/nav/jsf/pages/index.xhtml.

a. Margin of error of an estimate based on a 90% statistical confidence level. When added to and subtracted from an estimate, the range reflects a 90% statistical confidence interval bounding the estimate.

b. Ranks are based on the Congressional Districts' poverty rate estimates for 2013. Because of sampling variability, a District's rank does not generally statistically differ from other Districts with overlapping margins of error.

Author Contact Information

Thomas Gabe
Specialist in Social Policy
tgabe@crs.loc.gov, 7-7357